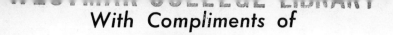

PUTTING FIRST THINGS FIRST

A Democratic View

Other books by Adlai E. Stevenson:

MAJOR CAMPAIGN SPEECHES, 1952

CALL TO GREATNESS

WHAT I THINK

NEW AMERICA

FRIENDS AND ENEMIES

ADLAI'S ALMANAC
edited by Bessie R. James and Mary Waterstreet

PUTTING
FIRST THINGS
FIRST

A DEMOCRATIC VIEW

BY

Adlai E. Stevenson

RANDOM HOUSE   NEW YORK

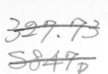
SECOND PRINTING

Publisher's Preface

When "Putting First Things First—A Democratic View" appeared in *Foreign Affairs* magazine in December, 1959, the editors of Random House agreed that this significant article by Adlai E. Stevenson should be republished in more permanent book form. After reviewing some of Governor Stevenson's other writings during the year 1959, we obtained his permission to include them in the book. These few selections from the work of but one year of his life—1959—reveal the clarity of mind and seriousness of purpose of this distinguished American.

We believe these selections are worth preservation and pondering by this generation of the friends of freedom and democracy.

Contents

PUTTING FIRST THINGS FIRST

A Democratic View

Putting First Things First

Peace is the most imperative business in the world today. It is the world's most universal desire and most powerful force. The mass of humanity seems to understand better than its rulers the idiocy of war and its mortal danger to the human race. Everywhere I travel the people appear to know that all their aspirations for freedom and dignity and a better life are going to be destroyed if mankind ever fights a modern war.

The United States has been the source of the most revolutionary and glorious concepts of human and political freedom. It had been my hope that in this revolutionary century the United States, which first split the atom, would be the tireless, fearless, indomitable leader of the cause of freedom from war. And I still think that to seize that role and pursue it with passion should be the top priority of American foreign policy.

Why haven't we really *led* the postwar world since the Korean War? Why are many Americans fearful that we have lost our sense of national purpose? Why is there confusion about intellectual and moral values? Why is

Reprinted by permission from *Foreign Affairs*, January, 1960, Vol. 38, No. 2. Copyright by Council on Foreign Relations, Inc., New York.

there a slackness about public problems and a wholesale retreat to the joys of private life? Why is balancing the budget a greater national concern than exertion, self-denial and hard work? Have we confused prosperity with security? Why is there a growing uneasiness over the contrast between a society like that of the Soviets which believes in its destiny and our own which seems to regard itself as fulfilled?

Personally, I think the trouble is not in the nation's energy, its will, or its nerve; and if wealth and comfort have softened us I am sure we are not yet beyond repair. The root of the trouble lies in this: the nation faces a series of massive changes in the world scene; they call for new ways of looking at the world, for new policies, for increased efforts. But since Korea our political leadership has not clearly and insistently acknowledged this fact. American policy has thus moved further and further away from the reality that surrounds us. Unchallenged by the realities, Americans have turned their energies and idealism to second-order business.

The main lines of American military and foreign policy are still those of 1947-1952. Although Messrs. Dulles and Eisenhower "crusaded" for a policy of "liberation" and denounced "containment" as "immoral," in operation their policy was to construct a chain of military alliances around Communism and to attempt to restrain the spread of Soviet power wherever it threatened. Oddly enough, Mr. Dulles' faith that Communism would disintegrate from its own internal contradictions resembled Lenin's conviction that capitalism would do the same.

But to win such an endurance contest we must have superior endurance. Yet instead of making massive efforts to improve or preserve the balance and to encourage attrition or benign change on the Soviet side, we emphasized conservative policies and fell behind on all fronts, while the Soviet Union, and other industrial areas, forged ahead at a rapid pace.

In short, while our Government adopted the Dulles foreign policy it did nothing to make it effective. Indeed, it was not long ago that Vice President Nixon saw something disloyal in my warnings about the Soviet rate of economic growth. (It is now double that of the United States!)

So for the most part the response of the United States to the great changes of this century has been only negative and defensive. An Administration which has defined its overriding task as keeping the budget down has dealt with them more with rhetoric than action. And unwillingness to acknowledge reality has led to a progressive erosion of the American stature on the world scene.

But it is not my purpose to indict the small aims and large fears of the Eisenhower-Dulles era. Things had to change, and I applaud the recent signs of more enterprise and flexibility in the conduct of our foreign policy. But I hope we Americans will not mistake Presidential goodwill tours for policy or serious diplomatic negotiation.

What are some of these realities which we must face in this age of many revolutions? The old colonial order has all but vanished. New nations—and new imperialisms—strive to fill the vacuum in a vast political revolution. Most of these new nations seek to bring their economies through the sound barrier of modernization in a few decades. This is the economic revolution. But they do so against the background of exploding population which will double the inhabitants of underdeveloped areas in the next generation. This is the biological revolution. Meanwhile, supersonic flight, atomic energy and the missile have opened up two opposite possibilities of equal magnitude—the exploration of planetary space, and self-extermination within the space of this planet. This is the scientific revolution.

What lies ahead of us in this bewildering century is invisible but it may be even more significant. In the past the North Atlantic nations dominated the world. But they could not control themselves, and their great world wars have diminished the power and influence of Europe. Now Russia and the United States have suddenly emerged as the two dominant powers. But already the brief day of two-power domination is passing and new centers of power are rising from old ashes in Asia. By the end of the century China and India will be industrialized, and China's population will be close to a billion. Then, as Europe becomes more unified, it too will reëmerge as a great center of power. And who can doubt that regional unification is going to take place in Latin America and emerging Africa?

So, this is not the beginning of the American Century, or anyone else's. It behooves us to face the reality that we Americans are not going to be alone at the center of the stage very long—and that modesty is always becoming. But if our tradition does not require us to be the world's boss, it does require us to keep alive and vigorous the great traditions of political freedom and legal order which underlie Western society.

To guide us through these uncharted seas, to comprehend and direct the prodigious forces now shaping the new world, is going to make heavy demands on our resources of wisdom, leadership, self-discipline and magnanimity. I would say that this reality belongs at the top of the list, because it has not yet been proved that democracy and the processes of persuasion can match the efficiency of central planning and dictatorship.

Multiple and universal change is thus the setting for policy in this age. Another reality we have been slow to admit is the present advantage this gives to the Communists. They did not invent the world's revolutions. All of these were—wittingly or unwittingly—launched in the West. But Communism, in itself a philosophy of change, exploits them world-wide. It uses all the anti-imperialist jargon and proclaims the brotherhood of mankind— Communist mankind. To our everlasting shame it has led the way through the frontiers of space and even pinned the Soviet colors on the moon. It proposes its own sweeping totalitarian planning as the only way out of economic stagnation, and the Soviet example of how to modernize and grow strong quickly has a powerful appeal to backward countries.

Mr. Khrushchev states his purpose plainly. He says, let's throw down our arms and we will beat you at peaceful competitive coexistence. He says that Russia will outstrip the United States in production and that one by one the neutrals will fall in line, while the Communist system spreads around the globe—and finally surrounds and isolates capitalism's last refuge in the United States. The Soviet planners expect that, as in China, the non-Communist regimes in Asia, the Middle East, Africa and parts of Latin America will be unable to solve the problems of modernization and economic growth and will turn to the Communist alternative, encouraged no doubt by Communist trade, aid and penetration.

This, I am convinced, is the route to world power which the Soviets now regard as the safest and surest. And in talks with Khrushchev both in his country and ours I felt that his confidence was genuine that history is working with him and that the system under which Russia became so strong so quickly is the system which other countries must follow. We refused to believe that Hitler meant what he said, to our sorrow. We should not do ourselves the same injury again.

To me the two most dangerous realities we now face are the multiplication of nuclear weapons and the disparity in living standards between the rich nations and the poor. I suggest we must meet these crises of our time in four major areas: First, we must end the growing gap between wealth and poverty. In doing so, we must, in the next place, create new supra-national patterns and institutions of cooperation. Thirdly, as long as nuclear weapons exist, the danger of their *use* exists. We must work for a disarmed world under law and organized police power— the only final answer to the threat of annihilating war. And lastly we must extend as far as lies in our power the concept of an open world. For it is in our acceptance of variety and differences, harmonized but not suppressed, that we in our turn work not only with the trend of history but in accord with the ingrained diversity of mankind. Our faith is that in the long contest the totalitarians will gradually be converted to our way of thinking rather than we to theirs. Our goal is not just to win a cold *war* but to persuade a cold *world*.

These are, of course, statements of high generality. We turn them into policy only by specific application and negotiation. Some aims we can pursue with like-minded nations, and we should proceed with them at once. Others depend on Communist assent and may take years of stoic negotiation.

The beginning of wisdom in the West, I think, is to have our own policy—not just a negative policy to stop the Communists, but a creative one that reflects our own vision of a viable world society and our own understanding of the revolutions through which we live. The voluntary ending of colonialism by most of the Western colonial powers, the Marshall Plan, Europe's moves toward unity and the various programs of economic aid, are creative innovations already to the West's postwar credit.

Once we know what we want, what our aims are, then we shall have to pursue them by every means with the same resolution and sacrifice that the Communists pursue theirs. It will not be easy to agree on them in view of the divisions among the Western powers, combined with the fact that Russia controls Eastern Germany and therefore the possibility of German unification. I suspect the hardest task will be to pursue our aims resolutely in common with our partners. For in "peacetime" democracies are at a particular disadvantage. Immediate domestic concerns take precedence over distant national goals. Too many selfish, thoughtless people prefer the easy option, and too many ambitious politicians prefer office to duty. But we cannot live by tail fins, TV and a "sound dollar" alone. Somehow we must lift our sights to the level of the tasks.

I will try to suggest some of our great tasks.

ECONOMIC DEVELOPMENT

The average annual income in the United States is more than $2,000 as against less than $100 for a third of the world's population. And the worst thing about this disparity is that the rich nations are getting richer and the poor poorer. Happily, there is, at long last, a growing realization here and among our friends that these are the decisive areas and that we must assist the underdeveloped peoples to advance to self-sustaining growth while preserving their independence and some hope of evolving a political democracy. Without an alternative to Communist methods of development, we face grim prospects indeed in poor countries where literacy is low, hunger high and the gap between resources and population widening.

Five conditions of success are, I think, clear. We shall be engaged on this program for at least forty years. We shall require a professional staff, with the languages and skills needed in this whole new field of activity. Informed opinion tells us that at least five billion dollars a year is needed—from all sources, public and private, domestic and foreign. We shall have to coordinate all aspects of the effort with other nations—not only investment but opportunities for trade, international liquidity and so forth. To get the maximum results the developed nations must all cooperate. The time has certainly come for other countries to share more of the common burden of assistance. In such circumstances the United States cannot expect to have full control of the use of all its expenditures for development purposes.

These five conditions are not yet fully understood, let alone accepted. There is still more than a hint that if the Communists would behave, the economic development program could be canceled. Partly as a result, our staffing policies are haphazard, our linguistic programs inadequate, and we are acquiring so many competing agencies, both national and international, that policies tend to be tangled and obstructed at the base and overlapping and bewildering in the field.

I regret that the Administration rejected the recommendation for a soft loan fund of about a billion and a half dollars for about five years. With Europe prosperous and dollars flowing to that area, Europe should mobilize an equivalent sum. With something like three billion dollars a year available for investment, with the West's great resources of skill and experience, and working with the World Bank, the Monetary Fund and the new International Development Association, it should be able to plan a concerted attack upon all aspects of backwardness—lack of capital, lack of skills, low reserves, single-crop exports and fluctuating world commodity prices.

It is difficult to establish priorities, but I believe there is general agreement that the whole political future of free Asia may depend on the success of India's great experiment. Certainly, too, the need is obvious for more rapid modernization and economic cooperation in Latin America. And the vision of a common market for the Western Hemisphere is even more exciting if it points toward economic federation in the whole non-Communist world.

For years I have urged that the United States put economic development on the same level of urgency as national defense, and press other advanced countries to join in a concerted effort. That in actuality we have no such joint program for world investment and growth springs in part from another weakness—our failure to develop an organic Atlantic community with common institutions and purposes. The ghost that has haunted every NATO conference for ten years is the ghost of the Emperor without clothes. The "wise men," committees and countless resolutions—all have spoken of NATO's positive tasks. We still have to find them. Worse, even the present measure of unity is being fretted away.

THE ATLANTIC COMMUNITY

Beneath the surface there are dangerous cross-purposes within our alliance. They are not to be overcome by ceremonial visits by Chiefs of State and by hasty diplomacy in preparation for meetings with Mr. Khrushchev.

The reconciliation of France and Germany is an historic achievement of postwar diplomacy. The Common Market is a creative effort to pass beyond narrow nationalism in the search for economic and social well-being and finally political union. But the price is high if France by moving closer to Germany moves away from Britain, and if the Common Market of the Six nations and the Free Trade Association of the Seven between them divide Europe into rival trading groups behind rising economic barriers which embitter not only commerce but politics as well. Nor do the divisions affect Europe alone. The frictions will be spread to Africa as a last divisive legacy of colonialism.

I believe it is a profound interest of American policy to see these nascent divisions overcome. We should urge the Six and the Seven to return to negotiation to mitigate tariff discrimination and liberalize trade. The United States and Canada should also cooperate systematically with the Six and the Seven to enlarge and use our influence vigorously to help solve in common the tough problems of commercial policy, including such questions as the stabilization of commodity prices in which the industrialized countries must of necessity take the lead. The last three or four years have demonstrated how even our own trade is becoming dependent upon European prosperity and how policies on each side of the Atlantic vitally influence the rest of the community. The unfavorable American balance of payments and fears for American reserves are already leading to a new isolationism, to creeping protectionism, to reduced foreign aid and to further divisions in our unity and strength. The Eisenhower Administration's "Buy American" policy in our lending will have negligible effect on our exports, and it repudiates the liberal trade and payments policy which we have been urging on our allies at the very moment they are adopting it.

Nor can we safely confront the Communist challenge with inferior military deterrent capability. If we fall too

far behind we may find Mr. Khrushchev's interest in negotiation has diminished. We must not tempt the Russians
with weakness and the only *safe* assumption for us to
make is that the Soviet Union may use force, as in Hun-
gary or East Germany, wherever there is no risk of general
war. As I have said to Mr. Khrushchev, equality of strength
and equality of risk are the only starting points for disarmament discussions.

In maintaining the military balance pending a reversal
of this senseless and bankrupting arms race, Western
Europe also should play an expanded role and assume a
larger burden. The cooperative control and use of atomic
weapons may now be the best way to prevent the divisive,
costly and inefficient duplication of nuclear capabilities.
Each one of the European nations cannot develop defenses capable of countering the Soviet threat, and should
not try. I don't see why we cannot distribute the nuclear,
the naval and the conventional burdens more econom-
ically and efficiently. The objective should be an inter-
dependent military system in which each nation's role
would be geared to its full technological and economic
capabilities.

We could recognize the fact of our economic, military
and political interdependence formally by the creation
of an Atlantic Council. With real powers it could formu-
late joint policies for sharing our responsibilities and
bringing about the genuine and equal partnership between the United States and Western Europe which our
successes in the past—notably the Marshall Plan—make
feasible and the greatest challenge we have ever known
now makes necessary.

I believe a North Atlantic Conference should be held
to outline new common policies for defense, disarmament, space exploration, monetary reserves, tariffs and a
larger economic sphere, and aid to the underdeveloped

areas, giving, I hope, new terms of reference to NATO and to other organizations. I think Europe should take the initiative toward creating some such new organization to deal with our great and growing problems and to promote more systematic Western cooperation.

Meanwhile, if our partners, including Japan, are to mitigate the harmful political pressures building up in the United States, a number of steps—toward which, I am glad to say, some progress has already been made—should be taken promptly.

Discrimination against dollar imports from the United States and all quantitative restrictions should be eliminated.

I have long urged that the nations whose economies the United States has helped to restore should assume a much larger share of the burden of aiding the underdeveloped countries.

The heavy task of maintaining large forces overseas aggravates America's balance of payments deficit; our European allies should now assume greater responsibility for the defense of the West.

While our balance of payments deficit may be a short-range problem, the liquidity shortage of the trading nations is not, and the West should move to correct this deficiency promptly.

A working cooperative Atlantic system would do more than enhance the basic strength of the West. It would demonstrate to other areas—to Latin America, for instance, or to free Africa—methods by which political autonomy can be combined with supra-national cooperation. In any case, the alternative is to see the centrifugal forces which are always at work between separate national entities pull us ever further apart. One thing is sure—we cannot deal with the Communist challenge divided and in disarray.

ARMS CONTROL

Most of all, a stronger Atlantic community will show the way to disarmament and peace. The frightful implications of modern war and the wasteful consequences of the nuclear stalemate are as visible in Moscow as in Washington. After my talks with Mr. Khrushchev, I have the feeling that some fixed Communist attitudes are changing; some, at least, of the Russian leaders seem to have concluded that the "capitalist" countries do not conform in all respects to the Marxist blueprint of misery and despair. Mr. Khrushchev has even changed his mind about the established Communist conviction that the United States could not cut arms spending without bringing on a depression. (I confess I get indignant when I listen to some of my fellow Americans who seem less confident than Khrushchev about our economy's resilience, especially when we have so many neglected tasks at home to which we could turn our energies and resources.)

The more the Communists see of the realities of Western society, the better for truth and so the better for us. Knowing something of the frightening darkness in which most Russians have to live, I favor the widest extension of exchange programs and cultural contacts. I would like to see the United States take the initiative in bringing Western and Soviet teams together in joint work. The principle of the Geophysical Year should be extended to a joint international Geophysical Commission. Other fields are Antarctic exploration and control, oceanography, medical and atomic energy research, exploration of outer space and even joint operations in certain areas of economic aid. Such communion of scholars and technicians could do more than awaken Communists to the reality of Western life and to the possibilities of an open world society. They could be forerunners of supra-national cooperation and organs of international control.

There is no difficulty in finding reasons why peace is so precious to the Russians after the desolation and destruction of two world wars. In addition, they now have much to lose, and their taste for the good life is rapidly developing. It is said that the Soviet defense effort takes about 25 percent of the national income as against 10 percent in this country. So for them another weighty reason for reducing the arms burden is to release more manpower and resources to improve the living conditions of the long-suffering Russian people and to strengthen the Soviet potential for economic competition and the paramount struggle for the uncommitted countries. It is likely that recent unilateral reduction of Soviet military manpower is dictated as much by the need for industrial labor as by changing defense concepts and the need to reduce military expense.

I am confident that some, at least, of the Russian leaders are anxious to halt testing and development of nuclear weapons before the danger becomes even more uncontrollable. But I wish I could be more sanguine that the Soviet Union was equally ready for the kind of inspection and control that would make possible any general arms reduction, let alone total disarmament. I suspect the conversion of the Soviet Union from a closed to an open society is still a long way off. But we should not hastily and cynically dismiss Mr. Khrushchev's disarmament proposals as propaganda and insincere. The question is not whether Communists are sincere but whether they are serious.

The root of East-West tension is fear. Whether it is rational or irrational, justified or not, hardly matters. It exists, and the peoples, especially Americans and Russians, have been indoctrinated with this fear of one another—these devil images—for years. Arms are a symp-

tom of the fears and tensions between nations. Therefore, the argument goes, disarmament is impossible until
political settlements have been reached and confidence
restored.

I disagree. I believe the nuclear arms race with weapons of mass destruction is a new element and in itself a
cause of tension. Of course, as I have said, we must try
everlastingly to improve relations by exchanges, negotiations, common projects, trade and agreements when possible. But fear will not vanish until the arms race is
arrested. We will have to proceed on all these matters
simultaneously. As Mr. Selwyn Lloyd of Great Britain
said in presenting the British plan for comprehensive
disarmament which preceded Mr. Khrushchev's: "If we
get political settlement it will make agreement on disarmament easier; and if we get an agreement on disarmament, it will make political settlement easier."

From what he said to me, I think Mr. Khrushchev
agrees too. And I am much encouraged by evidence from
many quarters that the Russians are genuinely worried
about the political and technical dangers and cost to the
U.S.S.R. of continuing the arms race indefinitely. Moreover, the United Nations disarmament resolution, agreed
to, *mirabile dictu,* by the United States and the Soviet
Union, recognizes that disarmament itself will promote
trust between nations and declares that disarmament is
the most important question facing the world today.

In short, it looks as though controlled disarmament was
back at the top of the world's agenda where it belongs.
I am sorry that the United States did not take and hold
the lead as I urged in the 1956 Presidential campaign.
Proposals by some of our leaders to resume nuclear tests,
together with hesitation and cynicism about disarmament
like the unfortunate announcement of "massive retalia-
tion" as United States policy, obscure our peaceful pur-

poses and help to validate the Communist propaganda that they are the peacemakers and we the warmongers.

Whether Mr. Khrushchev and his associates in the Kremlin really mean business depends on agreement to two main principles: a) that conventional and nuclear disarmament must go hand in hand, so that the balance of security between nations is not upset, and b) that progress at each stage must be subject to effective international control.

If universal and total disarmament should ever take place, a third need will arise: a supra-national force of some kind, as I have insisted to Mr. Khrushchev, in order that the sheer weight of such powers as Russia and the United States—or China—may not intimidate smaller neighbors. The composition, control and use of such a force, of course, present a host of further questions.

Meanwhile, pending the disarmament millennium, we must, as I have said, make good the deficiencies in our defenses to keep at least an equality of strength with the Russians. And I think it would be naïve to assume that they are yet ready to embark on the kind of positive cooperation in other respects which would establish real collective security. The conspiratorial tradition is very old and deep-rooted in Communist thinking, and when they talk of "peaceful competition," for example, I suspect that most Communists would include under that label political subversion, coups d'état, and even revolution under Communist party leadership.

Nevertheless, we may be approaching the time when the arms race with Russia can be arrested. Once a revolutionary regime leaves behind its adolescent fanaticism, risk and cost become powerful considerations. I believe they exercise genuine influence in Moscow today and that we should do what we can to encourage the trend.

CHINA

In Peking, however, I doubt if cost and risk are decisive factors. At this stage, pressure from "foreign devils," real or contrived, provides excuses for the austerity and brutal repression involved in the massive modernization. In this mood, China might conceivably be ready to risk a war which could mean disaster to its more prosperous Communist neighbor. Today, perhaps, Moscow can still limit Chinese aggressiveness by control over its military aid. But this influence will dwindle as China develops its industrial capacity, including atomic weapons. Has Russia therefore an interest in establishing some form of control now while her influence is still sizable? We do not know, but we must try to find out. And if we are going to make any important progress on disarmament, Russia will have to accept responsibility for bringing China in.

While there is little prospect of reasonable dealing with Red China at this time, it is apparent that Asians have become disillusioned and distrustful because of her imperialistic attacks on her neighbors and disregard for the "five principles of coexistence." I see hope in the fact that Mr. Khrushchev used Peiping as his sounding board when he warned Communists not to use force against capitalism. I see further hope in his proposal—ignored by Peiping—for an atom-free zone in the Far East. And even at this late date I suggest we explore with him the possibility of pacification in the area based upon a broad settlement of issues—including Formosa—by negotiation, not force.

On the Communist side, the concessions would include the extension to China of any system of international inspection of disarmament, ending the threat of force against Formosa and subversion in Indochina, a peaceful frontier settlement with India, free elections under United Nations supervision in Korea, and acceptance of the right of the inhabitants of Formosa to determine their own destiny by plebiscite supervised by the United Nations. On our side, concessions would presumably include an end to the American embargo on China's admission to the United Nations,* the evacuation of Quemoy and Matsu and the inclusion of Korea and Japan in the atom-free zone and area of controlled disarmament.

Perhaps neither the Russians nor we ourselves are yet prepared to talk in such concrete terms. Yet it is clear that no general control of disarmament has any value unless it includes China, and it is difficult to see how China can accept international control when it is not, formally, a member of international society. Moreover, as a member of the United Nations, Communist China, with a quarter of the world's population, would be more accountable to world opinion than as an outcast.

In the long run, the degree to which Russia is willing and able to moderate China's imperialistic designs will be a major factor in world peace. And it is likely that in its diplomacy as in its internal development Moscow is reaching the point where Mr. Khrushchev's peaceful coexistence with the West must grow into positive cooperation. Indeed I suspect the possibility of a new Russian-American alliance is not a wholly original idea in Moscow.

EUROPE AND THE MIDDLE EAST

The areas of the world where the interests and security of the great powers collide are the areas of tension where

---

* Admission to the United Nations should not be confused with diplomatic recognition by the United States for which there are better reasons for postponement.

negotiation must be concentrated if it is to be effective. I do not believe that local military blocs, directed against the Communists, always provide the answer. If we seek military clients, Russia can play that game, too, and more cynically. Moreover, she is not embarrassed by ties to the former colonial overlords. I do not mean that endangered countries should be left unprotected. The Eisenhower Doctrine is hardly more than a restatement of our commitment under the United Nations Charter and the Truman Doctrine to come to the aid of a victim of direct aggression. If the Soviets were directly to invade Iran— though it is not likely—American intervention would be unavoidable. And that is precisely why it is not likely. But Iran is no more secure because of military links with Pakistan, and the fate of Iraq shows how easily an unpopular alliance can be exploited to undermine a pro-Western regime.

I believe that we must look rather to disarmament and nonalignment, to political and economic collaboration, in the areas where Great Power interests collide, as in the Middle East. We still have a little time, for atomic weapons are as yet in the possession of only a few powers. Ten years from now, who knows how many local dictators may have them—to the detriment not only of our security but of Russia's as well. Here may be another common interest to explore. We might examine the possibility of an atom-free zone for the Middle East. We might also reconsider an earlier suggestion of an embargo on arms shipments into the Middle East—a plan which the Soviets have endorsed.

Neither Russia nor the Western nations have gained much from their recent policies of intervention in the Middle East. I suggest we now give organized nonintervention a trial. Some international problems are never solved; they just wear out. And the Arab-Israeli conflict may wear out before it is worked out. But meanwhile the United States should call upon the Soviet Union and everyone in the United Nations again and again to use their influence to harmonize relations between the Arab states and Israel and end this prolonged and useless hostility.

In the immediate future, however, the critical point of tension lies in Europe and Germany. There we have a perilous deadlock from which neither side can disengage without grave risk. On our side the fear is paramount that any withdrawal either from the exposed enclave of West Berlin or from West Germany would prove the first step in a general retreat from "positions of strength" in Europe. The end of the process could denude the Continent of American forces and undermine the defenses against a Russian advance to the Channel.

But the Soviets have comparable fears. The withdrawal of their troops to Russia would imperil the insecure Communist governments friendly to Russia and lead to the resurgence of a powerful and potentially hostile Germany. After suffering two shattering invasions in a generation, Russia's deep-seated fear of a rearmed Germany should not be hard for us to understand.

Russia's risk is probably greater than ours. After fifteen years of Communism, East Germany and Eastern Europe are still probably hostile to Russia. On our side, Communism has steadily lost ground. A Europe free to choose its destiny would not be Communist, and could be very anti-Russian. For this reason I believe we in the West play from strength in Europe.

I agree with Dr. Adenauer that the key to settlement in divided Europe lies in controlled general disarmament. The only satisfactory settlement for divided Berlin will be the unification of divided Germany. The road to unification lies through a reduction of fear in Russia and the West. And fear will subside only when there is progress toward disarmament with adequate controls. I doubt if we can reach more than provisional settlements or postponements of the problems of divided Europe until then.

But because a final breakdown over Berlin would end the new era of good feeling which Mr. Khrushchev has been cultivating and is as perilous to them as to us, some tolerable interim solution seems likely, compounded from the many proposals for an atom-free zone in Central Europe, scaling down of Berlin garrisons and occupation armies, security guarantees, etc.

A SENSE OF PURPOSE

In all of these great issues of international policy—whether they concern a world investment program for the underdeveloped countries, or methods of closer association with Europe, or the creation of communities of common work and interest with the Soviets, or the whole long arduous search for controlled disarmament—the first priority for the West is to recover the initiative. Out of a perpetually defensive attitude no lasting gains can come. Surely the West, which has been pre-eminently the challenger in human affairs since the dawn of the modern age, should not let the initiative slip from its hands.

Today, let us be clear, we do not have the initiative. Having caught up with us in weapons, it is the Soviet Union that is shouting about disarmament and peaceful competition; and it is the Soviet Union, strong and self-confident, that is now usurping the role of leader in the efforts toward peace. Mr. Khrushchev is the challenger—from outer space to inner Berlin. We react to his policies and conduct the world's dialogue on his terms. Between hasty improvisations and snap decisions we seem largely to have lost our own sense of direction.

We are ourselves to blame for this. The truth is that nations cannot demonstrate a sense of purpose abroad when they have lost it at home. There is an intimate connection between the temper of our domestic leadership and the effectiveness of American influence in the world at large. President Wilson gave a profound new direction to international thinking because he was a pioneer of the New Freedom at home. President Franklin Roosevelt's universal prestige as a liberal force in the world was deeply rooted in the New Deal, and this was the tradition carried on by President Truman in such great ventures as the Marshall Plan and the Point Four program. The link is no less vital today. If we cannot recover an aspiring, forward-looking, creative attitude to the problems of our own community, there is little hope of our recovering a dynamic leadership in the world at large. By our default as much as by his design, Mr. Khrushchev is enabled to continue dictating the terms of the world's dialogue.

I see little sign of any challenging approach in positive terms to our problems at the present time. In the most radical and revolutionary epoch of man's history, the dominant concerns of our leadership have been almost wholly defensive. We have not been urged and spurred on by the positive opportunities of world-building and nation-building inherent in our position as the most fabulously endowed people mankind has ever seen. On the contrary, our foreign policy has been dominated by fear of Communism, our domestic policy by fear of inflation. Economic assistance programs have been "sold" to the American people chiefly as a means of checking the Communists, never as our creative part in extending our technological revolution to the rest of mankind. The spur to our exploration of the solar system has not been our restless desire to extend the boundaries of human knowledge. It has been the irritation of seeing the Russians hit the moon first. Our interest in greater excellence in research and education flared up not because we want every free citizen to exercise to the full his innate talents and capacities, but because the Russians are producing more scientists and technologists than the West.

Even where we accept the Soviet challenge—as I assume we do in defense, science and education—our sense of urgency is not yet sufficient to override our obsessive fear that, in some way, in spite of having a gross national product of almost five hundred billion dollars and a per capita income almost twice as high as any other country's, we are staring bankruptcy in the face. How otherwise can we explain the fact that, with over twice the Soviet Union's national income, we have let them outpace us in arms, in space research, in proportional spending on education? How else are we to explain why our leaders see their most urgent task not in telling us the realities of our world and the duties and opportunities that lie ahead for a great and confident nation, but in warning us of all the insidious ways in which it can "spend itself" into penury?

The time has come to put an end to this unnatural timidity. There are other ways of securing a "sound dollar" than by stunting our national growth or—much worse—stunting our aspirations and our confidence in the great aims of our own society. Let us not measure our essential security, our standards of education and our public needs by "what we can afford." This is a static concept. What we could afford with a national income of two hundred and fifty billion dollars is not the same as our capacity today with nearly double the figure. Nor does it measure what we could afford if our rate of growth were purposefully increased.

Freedom is not an ideal, it is not even a protection, if it

means nothing more than freedom to stagnate, to live without dreams, to have no greater aim than a second car and another television set—and this in a world where half our fellow men have less than enough to eat. Today not rhetoric but sober fact bids us believe that our present combination of complacency and apprehension, of little aims and large fears, has within it the seed of destruction, first for our own community, and then for the larger hope that, as science and technology bring the nations inescapably together, freedom, not tyranny, will be the organizing principle of the society of man.

I believe the United States is ready for a new awakening and the achievement of greater goals. Within it are the moral and material elements of new purpose and new policy. It is the task of leadership to marshal our will and point the way. We had better start soon for time is wasting.

Our Broken Mainspring

It is hard indeed to pay adequate homage in words to a man whose own words were so fresh, so apt and fitting to the important issues of the day.

But I am encouraged by one fact. Dr. A. Powell Davies did not feel that his office as a minister of religion debarred him from comment upon contemporary problems. On the contrary, he saw that he could make his message relevant to his people only by showing it at work in the concrete issues of their daily lives.

I think of a story my grandfather Stevenson, a devout Scotch-Presbyterian, told about the preacher who was driving along a back road in the South when he espied a parishioner wearily clearing up a poor, stony field. "That's a fine job you and the Lord have done cleaning up that rocky field," he shouted. "Thank you, parson,"

A lecture inaugurating the A. Powell Davies Memorial Lectures, established in memory of Dr. Davies, for many years the much respected Minister of the All Souls Unitarian Church in Washington, D.C. It was presented in Constitution Hall, under the title of "The Political Relevance of Moral Principle," in Washington on Sunday, January 18, 1959, and has been somewhat abbreviated for this publication.

the man replied. "But I wish you could have seen it
when the Lord had it all to himself."

Dr. Davies believed that God is dependent on man,
as man is on God. He believed that the clergy above
all were responsible for making a reality of the bond
between God and man, and he was fearless in letting
his congregation and the world know the truth as
he saw it. He had a sensitive awareness of peril to the
individual in our day of bigness, of statism and conformity. Therefore he was impelled to fight for the oppressed
and the persecuted; to fight for equal justice for all and
the rights inherent in our citizenship. Ardently he de-
fended freedom of the mind, free speech, the right of the
dissenter to speak, the duty of the conformist to listen.
And his compassion was boundless.

It was the tardiness of the American social conscience
in understanding the severity of its ordeal, its contest
with authoritarianism that made Dr. Davies impatient,
that made him work so hard to awaken us to the perils.
He literally wore himself out trying to mobilize public
opinion, trying to induce every American to hold himself personally responsible for the preservation of freedom.

From the mountain of his vision, Dr. Davies constantly
proclaimed the political relevance of moral principle and
of religion as a "judgment of righteousness." From the
dusty plain of politics I would like in my turn to reaffirm
this relevance. I like to believe that there may be some
value in echoing testimony from a layman who has spent
his middle life in the press and confusion of great events
—in government service, in diplomacy and in politics.

There is a phrase of Dr. Davies that stays in my mind. I
do not know when I have heard a more terse and pregnant
summing up of our predicament. "The world," he said,
"is now too dangerous for anything but the truth, too

small for anything but brotherhood." This I believe to be in broad measure a correct estimate of the condition of human society, which is now capable, with a few hydrogen bombs, of extinguishing itself. Today we can all be killed by the same bombs or atomic fallout. In that sense we have attained a desperate physical solidarity. But moral and social solidarity in the family of man is still to be found.

Not so long ago I visited Dr. Albert Schweitzer in his primitive jungle hospital in French Equatorial Africa, and he told me that he considered this the most dangerous period in history. I said, "In contemporary history?" "No," he said, "in all human history." "Why?" "Because," he said, "heretofore nature has controlled man in the last analysis, but now man has learned to control elemental forces of nature—before he has learned to control himself."

Many of us seem, here in our country, to rely on some mythical God-given superiority of the white Western world to save us. And my concern is that there is more evidence that the Communists accept the reality of the human condition than we do.

It is impossible to spend weeks traveling around the Soviet Union, as I did this summer, without taking away an overwhelming impression of thrust and purpose in most aspects of Soviet life. The revolutionary ardor of the early days to be sure has cooled with time but even the very pragmatic political leaders seem to believe profoundly in the truth of their way of life and are quietly confident that it will sweep the whole world in time. I think they sincerely believe that their methods, their aspirations, their dreams, make up the final truth about the nature of man and society; that collective man in the collective state is the ultimate unfolding of human destiny, the end of history, the "far-off divine event" for which mankind has been in long travail, the vision of "all things made new" that has haunted men's minds ever since Christianity thrust into human thought the intoxicating ideal of a perfected humanity.

From this conviction, if I have not overstated it, flow two consequences. The first is that no effort, no dedication, no sacrifice is too great that may help to realize the Communist party's goals in Soviet society. The second is that no corner of humanity can be a matter of indifference to the Communists, because the whole human race is destined to become in time one communist brotherhood.

The energy, the drive, the dedication in the U.S.S.R. spill over into international affairs in ways that we are only now beginning to realize. In part, of course, this is the restless concern which all imperial powers must exercise, especially when the peoples they control are as restive and unreliable as the captive peoples in Russia's European empire. But Communist activity, planning and efforts in trade and aid are not confined to areas of Communist control. They are world-wide, and there is no corner of the earth's surface which the Russians think too insignificant for their attention, none.

All this we know—or begin to know. But I wonder how often we try to grasp the scale of dedication that lies behind it. Why should they be so busy? Why so much work and thought? Why such diversion of precious resources? Why such patience through every setback, such forward thrusts through every point of Western weakness? Heaven knows, we only want to stay home. Why don't they? Why do we never meet an isolationist Communist? These are some of the questions that haunted me when I confronted at first hand this iron, forceful, formidable way of life.

And I do not think that there is any doubt about the answer. Part of it is simply needed foreign trade. Part is fear, the search for security through friends. And part is the historical centrifugal forces in Russia which have been pressing outward for two hundred years—to the Pacific, the Balkans, the Middle East, the Straits, and so on. But the important thing is that the Soviet Russians believe in their truth, as the men of the Western world once believed in theirs. They, not we, are firing the shots that are heard round the world—and also the satellites that orbit above it. The fact that their faith is in many ways an evil perversion of the great propositions that once made the blood course in Western veins does not alter the fact that their tempo is dynamic and rapid, ours sluggish —even, I think, to ourselves.

Surely, the reason cannot be that we Americans have lost our vision of truth and brotherhood. No country on earth owes the sense of community more explicitly to the fact that it is united not by race or nationality but by fidelity to an idea. We were born "dedicated to a proposition" and our greatest leaders—the Jeffersons, the Lincolns, the Wilsons—were not great because they achieved purely American purposes, but because they were able to speak for humanity at large and extend their vision to the whole family of man.

Nor, I believe, can we find fault with the substance of what we have endearingly called the American dream. Its truths are still "self-evident." The possession of liberty and the pursuit of happiness—rightly understood—these have not been overthrown as the highest goods of human society. Indeed, the ferment of our freedom works inexorably and dangerously in the Communist world. No one can have visited Poland without seeing how little the Polish people really accept their servitude and how they look beyond their neighbors to the free world as the reservoir of power and of hope.

But, alas, on the basis of the record, one would hardly

suspect that the Western world possessed so powerful a weapon. Our talk—in diplomacy, in strategy, in aid and trade, in all of the intricacies of our world-wide relations—has been to a depressing degree purely defensive. We have offered aid not to help others but to shield ourselves. We have reacted to countless Soviet initiatives; acted on our own initiative barely at all. We watch the skies for other people's Sputniks and listen to the telegraph wires for other people's moves. Yet we are the free men of this universe; we are the children of liberty, the beneficiaries of unequaled abundance, and heirs of the highest, proudest political tradition ever known to man!

Why this lack of initiative? Why this paralysis of will? What have we done to our truth, our brotherhood— the supreme truth of freedom, the Christian truth of brotherly love? Have they failed? Or have we?

There is no more urgent duty than to discover why we have failed, if we have, and I think we have, and to get back into the arena, aspiring, striving, fighting, if you please, once more for what we believe. An examination of what you might call our collective conscience is to my mind far more important than particular projects or programs. You can have a perfect assembly of pieces in your watch, but they are worthless if the mainspring is broken. I am not worried about our various pieces—our technology, our science, our machines, our resources. But I am concerned, desperately concerned, about our mainspring. That it has run down, we know. But is it broken; is it broken beyond repair? In the last analysis, no question is worth more consideration in America today.

And I would like to suggest some of the ways in which it seems to me we have enfeebled the great central pulse of our freedom, the great truth of liberty, which, more than any other nation, we first set working in the modern world.

Goethe, who also lived through a crisis of freedom, said to his generation: "What you have inherited from your fathers, earn over again for yourselves or it will not be yours." We inherited this freedom we talk about so glibly. We seem unaware that it has to be remade and re-earned in each generation of man. One reason for this failure is, I believe, passing at last. In recent years we were stifled with complacent self-confidence. We believed ourselves dominant in every field. We talked of "the American Century." We forgot the ardors and the efforts that had given us a measure of pre-eminence. Complacency made us impervious to ideas, even the obvious idea that we are in danger. So we assumed that all we needed was to sit still and enjoy the "peace and prosperity" that was our right.

I believe that phase is now passing. Our foolish languor has been shaken, if not shattered. We are more ready to examine ourselves and our record. And it is a privilege of our society that every citizen should make his own inquiry. If I stress one or the other aspect of the problem, this is simply my angle of vision. You will have yours. The urgent thing is to feel the need for re-thinking and to set to work the ultimate energies of a free society— which cannot be done by the fiat of government but only by the troubled conscience of responsible men and women.

I believe—as I have said before—that we have confused the free with the free and easy. If freedom had been the happy, simple, relaxed state of ordinary humanity, man would have everywhere been free—whereas through most of time and space he has been in chains. Do not let us make any mistake about this. The natural government of man is servitude. Tyranny is the normal pattern of government. It is only by intense thought, by great effort, by burning idealism and unlimited sacrifice that freedom has prevailed as a system of government. And the efforts which were first necessary to create it are fully as necessary to sustain it in our own day.

He who offers this thing that we call freedom as the soft option is a deceiver or himself deceived. He who sells it cheap or offers it as the by-product of this or that economic system is knave or fool. For freedom demands infinitely more care and devotion than any other political system. It puts consent and personal initiative in the place of command and obedience. By relying upon the devotion and initiative of ordinary citizens, it gives up the harsh but effective disciplines that underpin all the tyrannies which over the millennia have stunted the full stature of man.

But of what use is escape from external restraint if given the opportunity man simply stunts himself? If freedom means ease alone, if it means shirking the hard disciplines of learning, if it means evading the rigors and rewards of creative activity, if it means more expenditure on advertising than on education, if it means "bachelor cooking" and "life adjustment" courses in the schools, and the steady cult of the trivial and the mediocre, if it means—worst of all—indifference, even contempt for all but athletic excellence in our educational system, we may keep for a time the forms of free society, but its spirit will be dead.

I believe we have had enough of adjustment, of conformity, of easy options and the least common denominator in our system. We need instead to see the "pursuit of happiness" in terms which are historically proven and psychologically correct. The dreary failure in history of all classes committed to pleasure and profit alone, the vacuity and misery accompanying the sole pursuit of ease —the collapse of the French aristocracy, the corruption of imperial Rome, the decline and fall of the resplendent Manchus—all these facts of history do not lose their point because the pleasures of today are mass pleasures and no longer the enjoyments of an elite. If we become a nation of Bourbons, numbers will not save us. We shall go their way, too. Vacuity and indifference are not redeemed by the fact that everyone can share in them. They merely restrict the circle from which regeneration can come.

I say this—I hope you will believe me—in no Puritan or pleasure-hating spirit. On the contrary, there is no boredom, no misery to equal the pursuit of distraction alone. We do not slip into happiness. It is strenuously sought and earned. A nation glued to recreation, to the television screen, is not simply at a loss before the iron pioneers of the new collective society. It is not even having a good time. No society has ever spent as much as we do on drink and tranquilizers. Can one argue that this is evidence of universal fun? I ran across a quotation from La Bruyère on the court of Louis XIV which struck me as relevant: *"Les joies sont visibles, mais fausses, et les chagrins cachés, mais réels"*—its joys are visible, but artificial, and its sorrows hidden, but real.

But perhaps this misunderstanding of the true nature of happiness and of the conditions of its pursuit is simply an aspect of something else—our misunderstanding of the real nature of freedom. I recall the words of the wise Judge Learned Hand, who warned us that freedom would not survive in our Constitution if it had already died in the hearts of the people. We shall not have a free society unless we have free men.

And how often do we reflect upon what this inner freedom entails? "Give me the man," cries Hamlet, "who is not passion's slave." But this is what we are in danger of becoming, slaves to a tyranny more intimate and inescapable than any that Stalin or Mao Tse-tung could impose. We can be made slaves simply by the clutter and complexity of modern living—which notoriously leaves no time for serious thought and offers every means of distraction so that we can avoid such thought. Between aircraft that take us everywhere more rapidly, newspapers that grow in weight and coverage, news that flashes round the globe, ceaseless and competitive entertainment, fashions—God help us!—that change from sack to trapeze and back again, we can fill up every "unforgiving minute" with enough trash and preoccupation to still forever the deeper voices of the soul. Like Matthew Arnold, we can

> ". . . see all sights from pole to pole,
> And glance and nod and hustle by,
> And never once possess our soul
>   Before we die."

How are we to defend freedom if, for the tyranny of external control we substitute the clattering, cluttering tyranny of internal aimlessness and fuss? This freedom of our souls, freedom at the profoundest level of our being, is not a gift to us by our contemporary way of life. On the contrary, much of this life is a direct conspiracy against it. And if we cannot—by a certain discipline, by readiness for reflection and quiet, by determination to do the difficult and aim at a lasting good—rediscover the real purpose and direction of our existence, we shall not be free. Our society will not be free. And between a chaotic, selfish, indifferent, commercial society and the iron discipline of the Communist world, I would not like to predict the outcome. Outer tyranny with purpose may well triumph over the inner, purposeless tyranny of a confused and aimless way of life.

I doubt if any society in history has faced so great a moral challenge as ours, or needed more desperately to draw on the deepest sources of courage and responsibility. Ours is the first human community in which resources are so abundant that almost no policies lie beyond our capacity for purely physical reasons. What we decide to do, we can do. The inhibitions of poverty —lack of resources, lack of capital, lack of power—do not hold us back. We can accomplish what we aim at. Thus, perhaps for the first time in the world, choice, not means, ends, not instruments, are decisive.

Then again we have proved—drably and dangerously —over the last decade that defensiveness is not a sufficient reason for action. All the policies we have pursued in self-defense have left us still on the defensive. But if we do not act from fear, we must find some other motivation. In free society there is no other alternative but to tap the vigor, the faith, the imagination of the people themselves. We must find out once more who we are, as the psychologists say.

But perhaps the most urgent reason why the quality of our moral response has become the decisive issue in politics is quite simply that most of the major problems of our day present themselves in moral terms, and are probably insoluble without some stirring of generosity, some measure of vision. Let me give you three instances. In the wealthiest nation in the world, at least five million families still live in squalid but remediable poverty. They are a minority. They do not have the votes to force the issue of their misfortune into the front rank of public issues. They depend, for remedies, upon the alert conscience of the majority. But how do we keep the conscience sensitive and alert? By concentrating on our own concerns? By adding the dishwasher to the television set to the air conditioner? By griping over taxes and attack-

ing that great bogey we call "the welfare state"? By closing our minds every time our shiny car takes us through
a slum? No—we shall have the dedication, the drive to
wipe poverty out of this rich land only if the well-to-do
majority of today do not repeat the selfish indifference
which, in many communities, has been the epitaph of
the well-to-do of yesterday.

Or take the issue of the rights and status of our colored
citizens. This is our small share of a world-wide problem.
The four hundred years of dominance of men of white
skin is ending. The vast colored majority of mankind
are seeking the opportunity and the respect which white
people have been lucky enough to enjoy for so long—
sometimes at the colored people's expense. But, within
this world-wide crisis, we in America, with our colored
minority, have a major role to play—for good or evil.
"The unfinished work" which Lincoln left us, of creating
a society in which all men can hold up their heads as
equals and self-respecting citizens, can never be accom-
plished unless there are enough white men and women
who resist to the core of their being the moral evil of
treating any of God's children as essentially inferior.

Nor is this simply a question of our own national community. I come back to the painful fact that the Communists show a world-wide concern which is largely
lacking among the men of the West. The whole human
race is their horizon. Their "brotherhood" is materialist,
collectivist, atheist, and we dislike it, but it embraces
everybody, and it is the framework of policies which take
the missionaries of their new order to the ends of the
earth. I say with all the emphasis that I can command
that we have no corresponding commitment to our fellow
man. For hundreds of years, we have preached the Chris-
tian promise of brotherhood, but today, when vanishing
space and scientific revolution have turned our planet

into a single neighborhood, the ideal means little in terms of concern or conviction, in terms of policy or of action.

Here we are in the Atlantic world, 16 percent of the world's peoples consuming 70 percent of the world's wealth. We cannot be indifferent to the moral implications of this gigantic gap. I do not know how we can gain a new perspective about the narrow world of plenty and of poverty in which we live unless moral insights of justice and compassion stir us to understand the privileged position in which we live.

We are not going to be stirred to action by our own needs. We are the cushioned, the protected, the fortunate minority. It is not the measure of our morals or the lesson of our history to be spurred on only by fear of Russian encroachment. What we have done has largely been from this motivation, and it has left us on the defensive. Our hope is to accept the implications of our own faith, to make concrete the image of brotherhood which we profess, to set to work to express our dedication in whatever effort or sacrifice the world's needs may dictate. And, if we must always think in terms of contest with the Soviets, let us bear in mind that the ability to create the good life for the greatest numbers will be decisive.

This age has been defined in many ways—as a time of conflict in ideology, as a time of ferment in technology, as a period of revolution in science, as an era when at last the means lie at hand to free mankind from the ancient shackles of pain and of hunger. It is all these things—but I believe the true crisis of our time lies at a deeper level. We have indeed conquered means and resources unknown at earlier ages. We have had thrown open to us frontiers of choice which would have left earlier ages stupefied by their scale and their scope.

But all this freedom and elbow room only thrusts onto us with more force the fundamental issue of the truth

that is within us. We can use our wealth, our capacity for
some vision of truth, some ideal of brotherhood, or we
can imprison ourselves within the selfishness of our own
concerns and the limitations of a narrow nationhood.
This is the dimension of our crisis.

You may argue that these qualities of dedication, of
selflessness, are pretty remote from the realities of politics.
They are all very well for private life, but what part can
they play in the rough and tumble of partisanship, of
primaries, conventions and election campaigns? Ambition, drive, material interests, political skills, the arts of
maneuver—all these, you say, have their part, but do not
let us pretend that the democratic process is primarily a
school of virtue or an arena of moral combat.

And yet, I wonder. It has been the view of great
philosophers and great statesmen that our system of free
government depends in the first instance upon the virtue
of its citizens. Montesquieu made virtue the condition
of republican government; Washington declared that it
could not survive without it. We have had a hundred
and seventy-five years of it and no one can deny that the
system has survived a remarkable amount of skulduggery.
In fact, it is probably a tougher system than its founders
imagined. Yet I believe they are right. For no democratic system can survive without at least a large and an
active leaven of citizens in whom dedication and selflessness are not confined to private life but are the fundamental principles of their activity in the public sphere.

Naked interest and ambition will carry a lot of people
naturally and inevitably into politics. We do not need
societies for the promotion of lobbies. Interests, good and
bad, will promote themselves. Nor, in any generation do
we lack politicians whose only principle of action is the
advancement of their own career—the starry-eyed oppor-
tunists and all the other eager men in a hurry to the top.

But into what state must politics degenerate if that is all we find active in the political arena? That and sectional interests played upon by personal ambitions? There have been such periods, but our democratic system survived them because such epochs were followed and cleansed by periods of disinterested reform.

But there has never been any disinterested reform without disinterested reformers. And here we come to the essential contribution made by dedication and selflessness to the public good. No one ever did any good in politics without readiness for endless hard work—for the grinding, boring, tedious work, as well as the glamorous, high-sounding, headline-hitting work. The painstaking hours collecting the facts, the hours in committee and conference, the hours in persuasion and argument, the hours of defeat and disappointment, the hours of disgust and revulsion at the darker sides of human behavior—these cannot be supported without energy and devotion. No reform comes easy; even the most obvious will have its entrenched enemies. Each one is carried to us on the bent and the weary backs of patient, dedicated men and women.

They are not only dedicated in their readiness to give energy and work to the cause; they must also have sufficiently clear sight and open minds and hearts to see the need for reform in the first place. But clear sight or an open heart for the needs of others is again something that hardly "comes naturally." We have so many needs of our own—our families, our jobs, our homes, our fortunes, our prospects. We are hemmed in with needs and interests, weighty, urgent, honorable, human needs and interests, even if they are exclusively our own. It takes an extra dimension of vision to see beyond our inner circle of personal interest. Most people, most of the time, do not possess it, that extra dimension of vision, which is one reason why self-regarding interests make up so much of the stuff of politics. And this, I suppose, is why the men and women of genuine, imperturbable public spirit seem so few and far between.

I sometimes think there is a danger of this element of vision vanishing almost wholly from our political life. In the main we are so comfortable; so many evils of the past have shrunk in size and almost out of sight. At the same time, people marry much younger; they have larger families and are profoundly involved in earning a living, making careers and safeguarding the future of their children. It is more difficult, they say, to give time to public affairs when private life is so urgent and so absorbing.

Yet is it, I wonder, more urgent and absorbing than it was a hundred years ago, when men not only married young, had large families, built up careers, but also opened up the new frontiers, created new cities out of the wilderness and gave to new states and communities the framework of active political life?

If one reads the story of young Abraham Lincoln, it is hard to believe that his struggles as a young lawyer, his difficulties as a young parent were less than those of young men today. Yet there was no time when the deepest issues of the day did not occupy his mind or the call of statecraft make itself heard above the claims and clamor of everyday life. Nor was he alone or exceptional. Stephen Douglas' life was no different. The prairie towns were filled with earnest, active citizens deeply, profoundly concerned with the great issues of a nation "half slave, half free." When the multitudes gathered, a hundred years ago, to listen in rapt attention for hours to the Lincoln-Douglas debates, had they fewer responsibilities and duties than the citizens of today to many of whom the great issues of politics seem to be most usefully conveyed in a fifteen-second television flash of subliminal advertising?

Is it not possible that the pressures of personal responsibilities are not greater but that the dedication and selflessness needed to discern and to influence public issues have shrunk? In a century in which so many of the mentors of the public mind—from the psychiatrists to the ad-men—speak to us in terms of "what we owe ourselves," may there not indeed have been a slackening of devotion compared with those days, not so long distant, when what man owes to God and his neighbor was a common theme of public discourse?

If so, this is a dangerous hour for our politics and for government by consent of the governed. For at no time have so many of the great issues of the day demanded clear, real moral vision to bring them into focus—the vision, if you please, of A. Powell Davies, who loved the truth and believed in man's capacity and right to govern himself.

The Public Responsibility of Private Power

I understand that this audience, the Institute of Life Insurance, represents the largest aggregation of investment capital in the world. Well—this is a most unusual environment for a Democrat! And I must say that there have been occasions in the past when I would have welcomed even more the attention and good will—and contributions!—of businessmen of such influence and affluence.

I know it is customary at meetings of this kind to tell you how important, useful and wise you are. That wouldn't be hard to do with the life insurance business, which has pioneered in the development of greater economic security for our citizens and advanced and improved our housing, education and health.

But I want to talk not about our virtues and triumphs but about our faults and failures. For in a matter of days we enter a new decade. Just as a hundred years ago, on the eve of the Civil War, we entered the decade of the '60s that proved decisive to our republic, so in this cen-

Address given at luncheon of Institute of Life Insurance, Waldorf-Astoria Hotel, New York City, December 8, 1959.

tury we are entering the same decade—on the eve of trials equally decisive. Therefore it seems to me not a time for uncritical self-congratulation but for critical self-examination. Shaw wrote: "The more things a man is ashamed of, the more respectable he is." Well, I don't think we are as respectable as we like to think.

I don't think we are shocked by the gross inadequacies of our schools, or by our scientific achievements lagging behind the Russians'. I don't think we are ashamed or really much concerned about our decaying cities, about our neglected resources or the infirmity of our defenses, or about the implications of the growing disparity of living standards between the rich and the poor nations, or that America's stature in the world has been declining while the crisis is mounting.

And, finally, in the face of the most powerful and dangerous challenge our capitalist economic system and our democratic political system have ever confronted, I have seen little awareness of the public responsibility of private power.

But the steel strike dramatizes the fact that we are at the end of an era. Everybody is agreed that this cannot happen again; that the public interest is the paramount interest, and that irresponsible private power is an intolerable danger to our beleaguered society.

Our American tradition has been to disperse power and trust to luck to make power responsible. James Madison, in the *Federalist* No. 10, found safety from factions in having a great many of them, fighting over a large territory. But in order to have any confidence that if enough centers of power contend they will make one another responsible, we must attribute to Providence a greater interest in the welfare of the American people than either our history or our merits would seem to justify.

The time has come for us as a people, as a community learning together, to learn how to assume conscious control of our destiny. If a society is to be free and just, all power in it must be made responsible. We are certain of this when it comes to governmental power. When the Constitution was framed, government and the individual were the only two entities in society. Government was the one with the power. Now other centers of power may have a more direct and drastic effect on the individual and on the life of the country than any eighteenth-century government could have hoped to have. This raises new constitutional questions. Where private groups— like big business and big labor—are performing public functions, they must be held to public responsibility. And one may forecast with some certainty that the Supreme Court will increasingly hold them to this responsibility.

But are the alternatives always between governmental control and letting private power run wild until it is checked by collision with other private powers? Are there other instruments of criticism and correction?

Although I see few signs that the universities, the media of communication, and the professional associations are interested in becoming centers of independent criticism, there are some indications that we may eventually develop new institutions for the purpose. The recommendation of the Commission on the Freedom of the Press that a continuing agency be established to appraise the performance of the media is being actively debated. Senator Cooper has introduced a bill calling for a national advisory council on education. The Center for the Study of Democratic Institutions reports the need for an organ of criticism with regard to the economic order. There are some stirrings among scientists, engineers and medical men that may give us some hope that these professions may ultimately try to give some reasonable direction to the greatest irresponsible power at large in the world, the power of technology.

And if private power is to be made responsible, we shall have to look to the centers of power, like the business community, to bring about this result. Businessmen will have to get over their neurosis about Government, for Government has a positive duty to see to it that business is directed to the common good. The same is true of labor. To the extent to which labor and management see to it that their activities are directed to this end, direct intervention in their affairs by Government may be avoided.

But in September it proved necessary—for the first time in our history—for Government to establish controls over the internal affairs of the labor unions—their constitutions, their elections, the administration of their offices—because of the irresponsibility of a comparatively few labor leaders. This was a failure not just for the unions, but for democracy. The system is weaker today than it would have been if labor had done for itself what Government has now had to do for it.

And now there is this bitter, stubborn failure of private responsibility in the steel industry.* Although the public has been barred from knowing what is going on, it now appears that the crucial issue is not wages, but rather the handling of the problems arising from automation. And apparently both sides are insisting on virtually absolute control over these decisions, without regard to the cost to the country.

The basic failure was far deeper than the fact of the strike itself. Thoughtful men, who have championed col-

* NOTE: At this time the steel industry had been shut down by a stubborn labor-management dispute for almost four months and had only recently resumed production under an 80-day injunction.

lective bargaining as a keystone of a free economy, are now voicing concern about its capacity to cope with the problems of the technological revolution—at a time when America cannot pay the price of nation-wide stoppages in its basic industries.

By the end of January—unless earlier settlement is reached—the country will again be exposed, with no protection, to a steel strike. And in the spring the question will be whether the railroads will be operating or not.

The impression created around the world by the spectacle of such failures in our vaunted democratic capitalist system is lamentable. I suspect the country will no longer accept this state of affairs. And if there are more stoppages Congress may be expected to reflect the public temper in legislation which would not only stop strikes but might stop or seriously cripple collective bargaining too. The most likely prospect would be some form of compulsory arbitration, limited to the case itself. But our experience with compulsory arbitration is that it so undermines private collective bargaining that the Government becomes the arbiter for all labor disputes, and then for price determinations as well.

So one will hope for a settlement before further stoppages provoke extreme remedies. But it is now apparent that the emergency disputes provisions in the Taft-Hartley Act do not work and that a new and reasonable law is needed.

I hope you will forgive my speaking of this last point in personal terms. "I told you so" has always seemed to me a demeaning phrase. But with your indulgence I want to quote from a speech on Labor Day, 1952, in Cadillac Square in Detroit, by a then candidate for President:

New methods must be found for settling national emergency disputes. . . .

We cannot tolerate shutdowns which threaten our national safety, even that of the whole free world. The right to bargain collectively does not include a right to stop the national economy. . . .

All the Taft-Hartley answer boils down to is that in national emergency disputes employees shall be ordered to work for another 80 days on the employer's terms. . . .

What we need is a . . . law that will provide for investigation and reporting to the public on the issues involved, one that will provide for more effective mediation between the parties . . . [Because these emergency cases are always different] the Congress should give to the President a choice of procedures when voluntary agreement proves impossible: seizure provisions geared to the circumstances; *or* arbitration; *or* a detailed hearing and a recommendation of settlement terms; *or* a return of the dispute to the parties. . . .

If there is excuse for this anecdotal intrusion it is only in the fact that I would propose today substantially what I did then—except a little more so.

The "choice of procedures" approach still seems to me the right one. I think of it as essentially a mediation approach—but with real teeth in it, with the opportunity afforded for effective assertion of the public interest, and —if I may use the term here—with the inclusion of an "insurance policy" covering the possible risk of mediation failure, with the public named as the beneficiary.

I would add one proposal to my 1952 suggestion—the President should have authority to convene a special public board—a Board of Public Responsibility—well in advance of the strike date in any key industry, perhaps as listed by Congress. The Board would meet with the parties to the dispute; it would express the public interest to the parties, keep the President advised, and perform whatever mediation functions appeared advisable. Its effectiveness would be immeasurably enhanced by the parties' knowledge that the Board's final responsibility—if its efforts at mediation should fail—would be to recommend to the President what further action should be taken. The possible forms of this further action, the "choice of procedures," would include, to avoid any party's confident reliance on being "taken off the hook," the possibility of *no* further action—assuming the situation permitted this.

With such a law it is likely that no case would ever get to the final stage requiring the ultimate Presidential action. But if it did—if the parties were unable or unwilling to resolve their dispute, to exercise responsibility consonant with their power—then I would see no reasonable objection to requiring that the dispute be taken out of their hands entirely; that the President be authorized in that case to require in one form or another that production be continued while the dispute was resolved by process of reason rather than by subjecting the economy to grievous injury.

I have no illusions about this proposal. It will be objected to on the ground that it intrudes the Government into these cases at too early a stage. I think not. It was one thing to expect the public to accept the results of collective bargaining when that result represented the "decentralized decision making" of a thousand different sets of negotiations. But with the development of industry-wide bargaining, decisions affecting the entire economy are made by a small group of men sitting at a single table, and the public has no alternative to accepting those decisions. I think it is entitled to be represented at that table in the restricted sense I have suggested.

Also it will be said that this proposal involves a denial of the rights of labor and management to strike and to shut down a basic industry. It seems to me that this, too, is a legitimate and necessary implication of the decision to resort to industry-wide bargaining. The greater the power, the larger the responsibility. When the public is denied alternative sources of supply it is entitled to demand that the supply not be shut off. It was in a similar context of labor-management strife that Mr. Justice Brandeis once said: "All rights are derived from the purposes of the society in which they exist; above all rights rises duty to the community."

More and more, the right of the bargainers to disagree and to stop working and producing in order to force agreement, is affected by the blunt truth that the American economy must compete today with an economy made dangerously effective by its refusal to pay any of freedom's costs—like a strike.

All these changing circumstances demand fundamental changes in the collective bargaining process. They will mean, I suspect, increased use by labor and management of various forms of continuous bargaining, in place of the present practice of concentrating all bargaining in the brief periods just before old contracts expire, while a strike bomb is set and ticking.

Finally, let me repeat and emphasize the importance of the fact that our economy, and the society it serves, will be weaker by whatever degree it is necessary for Government to intrude upon the settlement of labor-management disputes in order to make private power responsible.

But I wish our failure to display to a watchful, skep-

tical world the fullest wisdom and responsibility of democratic capitalism was confined to labor-management relations.

Increasingly in the past eighteen months I have become
puzzled by the rising chorus of fear about this great and
powerful economy. When a $500,000,000,000 annual in-
come is in sight; when we have the highest per capita income in human history; when we have weathered three
recessions without a decline in consumer income; when
catching up with American productivity has even become
the—curiously un-Marxist—goal of our rivals, the Russians, our leaders tell us we can spend on space research
only half what we spend to store a single year's surplus
crop; we cannot afford to spend proportionately on education what the Russians spend, on welfare what the Scandi-
navians spend, on arms, I'm told, what the Chinese spend.
We have half the free world's gold, and only twice since
1945 have we had an adverse balance in our international
payments, yet we attach with panicky haste the "Buy
American" strings to our loans while asking everyone
else to end their trade restrictions.

What is one to make of it all?

On the one hand, we are the wealthiest people in history; on the other we teeter on the edge of bankruptcy.
With goods fairly running out of our ears, we moan about
the dangers of inflation.

But, of course, the issue is a phony one. When our
political and business leaders warn us that we are "spending ourselves into bankruptcy" they have only one kind
of spending in mind—public spending derived from
tax money or official borrowing. Nobody cries "reckless
spending" when perfectly good office buildings on Park
Avenue with years of life ahead of them are pulled down
to make room for new ones carrying higher rents and
higher profits. The charge of spending is hurled instead

against attempts at the other end of the same avenue to pull down ghastly tenements and rehouse families with the elements of human decency. There is no outcry about business expense accounts that equal in a year what a primary-school teacher can earn in a decade. Who asks what cost to our economy day by day is added by including in the cost of every product the packaging and persuasion to buy what in many cases people do not really want? It is said that we spend more per head of population on advertising than on schooling.

Where, then, is the waste? Surely not in the public domain.

In short, what the prophets of bankruptcy and collapse really mean is that all government expenditures must be held to a minimum while the flood of private consumption goes up unchecked, even if the consumption is of marginal human value. There is more here than a matter of priority and value. For it is precisely in the public domain that the Communists present their most dangerous threat. To refuse to meet the challenge in the area of government spending is ideology in reverse. Unless we are prepared to spend not what we can "afford" but what we need in such areas as defense, economic aid, education and basic research—to name only the four chief areas of Communist challenge—it is not just our free enterprise system that we are putting in jeopardy, it is the survival of free society itself.

I think we are evading this issue. I think we have underrated the Soviet challenge. Their atom bombs came long before we expected. Sputnik was an ugly surprise to us. Now they have pinned their colors to the moon, and even sent us photographs of its back side. Four years ago I often warned about the implications of rapid Soviet economic growth. It makes no difference that Vice President Nixon broadly hinted that therefore

I might be a disloyal American. But it does make a difference if we are still making the mistake of under-estimating our rivals—perhaps as an easy escape from the disagreeable fact that public spending, far from fall-ing, very probably ought to increase; that taxes, far from falling, may have to be higher, at least until disarmament or an accelerated rate of economic growth gives us ade-quate resources.

The point is that business carries a heavy share of the burden of foresight, understanding and leadership not to put the last least triviality of private spending ahead of public needs in priority and esteem. Public spending in defense and research must have priority because sur-vival depends upon it. Public spending on education, on health, conservation and urban renewal must have prior-ity because the dignity and grace of our free way of life depend upon it.

And there is another priority—the question whether as a community, we, the wealthiest society known to man, can keep our spiritual self-esteem and offer the poor underdeveloped countries an alternative to Communism as a method of economic modernization.

Regardless of the Communist competition in these decisive areas, we have to go no further than the Chris-tian basis of our nation's ethic to know how this issue will be decided. While we double and treble our standards of life, the meager living of nearly half our fellow men on this planet threatens to diminish further. For example, the discrepancy between India's per capita income of $60 and our own, about $2,000, confronts us with a job already as great as the gulf between Dives and Lazarus, and growing wider.

Now that Asian attention is riveted on the President's journey, how incalculable might be the effect if we were to choose Delhi to announce a new and sustained Western effort to aid world growth and world investment. For in India live nearly half the inhabitants of the emergent areas.

I have talked to you leaders of a great essential business about our failures because I have seen little sign of any challenging, positive approach to the great problems of our time. In the most radical and revolutionary epoch of man's history, our dominant concerns seem almost wholly defensive. We are not spurred on by the positive opportunities of world-building and nation-building inherent in our position as the most fabulously endowed people mankind has ever seen.

On the contrary, our foreign policy is dominated by fear of communism, our domestic policy by fear of "inflation." Economic assistance programs have been sold chiefly as a means of checking the Communists, never as our creative part in extending the technological revolution to the rest of mankind. The spur to our exploration of the solar system and scientific research has not been our restless desire to extend the boundaries of human knowledge. It has been irritation with the Russian achievements. Interest in greater excellence in education flared up not because we want every free citizen to exercise to the full his innate talents and capacities, but because our rivals are producing more scientists and technologists.

Can't we put an end to this unnatural timidity and defensiveness? Everyone will agree that a sound dollar is essential. But there are other ways of securing it than by stunting our national growth or—much worse—stunting our aspirations and our confidence in the great aims of our own society.

So let us assess our needs—our need to maintain equal-

ity of military strength, until controlled disarmament
takes its place, our need for better education, our need
for wider research, a greater thrust into outer space, our
need for decent cities where segregation and delinquency
give ground in the wake of redevelopment and renewal,
our need to conserve our national resources, above all,
water.

All these needs—domestic, foreign and military—will
cost more money, at least until we can make some progress with disarmament. But keeping the budget down
isn't as imperative as keeping our heads up.

I think our needs could be covered by existing tax
rates at higher levels of economic growth. But I am sure
that if our political leadership defines the tasks with
clarity and conviction, we will approve what is necessary
to fulfill our national purpose whatever the sacrifice—
higher taxation in years when the private economy is running at full stretch, for instance, budgetary deficits in
times of slack, restraint upon wages and profits to slow
down inflationary pressure, less emphasis on private
rights, and more on public responsibility.

But the recompense will be to see American society
once more the pace setter in human affairs, to see freedom once more the great challenger on the human
scene. For this, surely, is the crux. An attitude of un-
adventurous conservatism cannot stand for long as the
creative image of freedom. I tremble for our future—
and for the world's future—if growth, thrust, initiative
and the vast new frontiers of science are felt to be the
prerogative of Communist discipline and drive—if "the
shot heard round the world" has been silenced by the
shot around the moon.

Today not rhetoric but sober fact should bid us believe
that our curious combination of complacency and apprehension, of little aims and large fears, has within it the

seed of destruction first for our own community, and then for the larger hope that, as science and technology bring the nations inescapably together, freedom, not tyranny, will be the organizing principle of the society of man.*

* NOTE: The opinions Mr. Stevenson expresses in the closing paragraphs of this speech were also incorporated in a published article, "Putting First Things First," which appears as the opening selection in this book.

Businessmen Who Think Greatly

Alfred North Whitehead once said: "A great society is a society in which its men of business think greatly of their function." Are American businessmen today "thinking greatly"? I say no; and thus I am cast in the role of critic, setting out to state bluntly what seem to me to be the obligations, especially the unmet obligations, of the business community to the community at large.

I appreciate fully my danger. A request for criticism is not always to be taken at face value, and the critic is not always popular as I have some reason to know. But I am not unaccustomed to the task.

I have been a businessman's lawyer most of my life and have had some trouble "thinking greatly" myself, let alone telling my friends and clients how to think greatly about the future of society. But surely there is serious unease in the nation and the world, and it is time for *some* thinking, difficult as it may be. None of us is satisfied

Reprinted by permission from *Business Responsibility in Action*, published by McGraw-Hill Book Company, Inc., New York. Originally this paper was delivered at the Harvard Business School on June 6, 1959, at the concluding session of the National Business Conference.

with the way things are going; we are surrounded by both troubles and opportunities.

And the businessman, although he has lost much of his former influence, is still "central" in and indispensable to the American and world systems. So it is imperative that he, of all people, "think greatly," that he assume a more objective and influential role in the larger concerns of the new equalitarian society that is emerging here and everywhere in this age of revolution.

I think of the prayer of a little English boy in World War II: "God bless Mother and Daddy, my brother and sister, and save the King! And, oh God, do take care of yourself, because if anything happens to you we're all sunk!" Please don't think that I am equating business and God. I'm a Democrat and you have not fooled me! But the pivotal position of business and the business manager in our society must be obvious to any serious student of our system.

How have businessmen done so far in these respects? My answer is "not well enough." The great changes that have taken place in America in the past fifty years have been effected most of the time over the protest of the business community. Business fought bitterly, for instance, against increasing graduation of the income tax; against the Social Security program and the minimum-wage law; against unemployment compensation and the strengthening of collective bargaining; against enlarged housing and educational programs; against TVA and other natural resource developments; against farm price protection; against foreign aid.

The plain fact is—without arguing the "rightness" or "wrongness" of any one of these policies—that in the judgment of the community, American business has been wrong, shortsighted, and more interested in profit than people, in dollars than ends. Two hundred years ago

Rousseau said: "As soon as public service ceases to be the chief business of the citizens and they would rather serve with their money than their persons, the State is not far from its fall."

It is not easy to find an explanation for this record of failure. I think the business community is the victim of an intellectual time lag. In the span of about fifty years we have altered the whole physical apparatus of our lives. We have conquered space, split the atom, lengthened life, doubled the world's population and launched the interplanetary adventure. Yet, although everything is changed, we all sense that our thinking about the aims, scope and performance of our economic system has not kept pace; that at least in some degree stereotypes, ideology, prejudice, even myths, have taken the place of that re-examination and self-analysis from which no human society ought to be long divorced. To a considerable extent, the businessman is both the victim and the perpetrator of this unhealthy situation.

Enough of the obvious. The important fact now is that in these times of violent change the nation desperately needs to have the American business community reoriented and assured of itself and its direction once again. We face great thickets of tangled dilemmas which cannot be solved without great thinking and mighty actions in which the business community must play a leading role. Taken together—and I hope I do not sound melodramatic—these problems are placing the American system on trial for its life.

Many of the issues pose direct challenges to our economic system, for which the businessman is primarily responsible; all of them have economic overtones. So a realistic re-examination of our economic system and its state of readiness is a responsibility business and industry cannot, must not, evade or postpone.

Let me suggest a few of the major questions in the economic sphere which are lodged firmly in the laps of American business managers, and which demand a new look at our economic machine.

(1) The most important is the disparity in living standards over the world—measured roughly by average income of $2,000 per year in North America as against $100 or less for more than half of the world's population. And the rich are getting richer and the poor poorer all the time.

(2) The Communist world-wide economic offensive, which gives us cause for greater concern than does Communist military strength. To maintain the balance of power, if for no other reason, the West will have to make a greater effort to provide an alternative to communism as a technique of change and growth in the vast underdeveloped areas. Brains and sensitivity are as important as money.

(3) The huge social-capital requirements at home for education, housing, health, urban renewal, resource development and the like.

(4) The control of inflation without depression.

I could go on; but I hope this brief list of our larger concerns suggests that the priorities, values, philosophy and emphases in our society must be adjusted to some tough realities. Our traditional standards and goals—an ever higher standard of living here at home and an ever more comfortable life for ourselves—will not do for this age. If we persist in them, they will prove inadequate to the times. And the road of history is marked by the whitened bones of civilizations which were based on a set of goals that the passage of time had made obsolete.

Can it be done in peacetime? Can a society wrench itself free from a set of values that have become a straitjacket and reclothe itself in more suitable fashions? Even under the threat of a powerful opponent and of mankind's self-annihilation, can people perform this mighty action and the great thinking which must underlie it? Frankly, I do not know. But I do know that to see that we do is the very top responsibility of business—yes, and labor, and all the rest of us, too.

One of the parts of our new garment of values must be sustained, substantial economic growth. To achieve the level of growth we need, we may have to make some sacrifices in taxes and prejudices. We may have to turn from the temptations of more leisure and less work, of simple routine and standardization, to irritating, demanding innovation instead. But it is clear that we cannot meet the relentless foreign and domestic challenges without sustained economic growth.

Superficially, our concern with economic advance arises from the loud words of Mr. Khrushchev, who is voicing the changed direction of the Marxist attack. Since the Communists can no longer aim their barbs at poverty and misery in our system, they must find some other target. Curiously enough for a revolutionary, antibourgeois movement, they are now saying that our way cannot produce as high a living standard as rapidly as theirs can. By the very nature of a free enterprise economy, they tell us, we cannot grow steadily or hope to keep pace with Communism's surging advance of 7 percent or 8 percent a year. "We will bury you," says Mr. Khrushchev, "not under hydrogen missiles but under a flood of production which will finally prove to the Russian people and to the world at large that 'we can do everything you can do better,' and do a lot of things in addition which you cannot do at all." And to prove his point, Khrushchev is driving the Soviet Union to catch up with America, and has proclaimed this as his main domestic aim.

Here then is the new challenge—the challenge represented by the competition of sustained growth secured by government direction. The Communist performance since the war—both in Russia and China—is formidable enough for us to take the challenge seriously. We can no longer take our own productive, scientific and technological superiority for granted.

But this gauntlet is not the real—or, at least, the only —reason that we must devote ourselves to economic growth. We have demonstrable human needs unsatisfied at home and heavy obligations overseas. Consequently, the Communists' challenge—that they and only they know how to grow rapidly and indefinitely—becomes relevant not only in itself but also in terms of the great contest of the future. We must grow for our own sake because of three facts:

The first is our rapidly expanding birth rate. We are growing by about 2 percent every year, an increase as large as India's. This wave first hits our homes and cities, then our schools, and at last our labor force where, when combined with a 3 percent increase in productivity, it will call for more jobs at a rate approaching 5 percent a year.

Secondly, we have a long backlog of undone tasks left by the depression, then the World War, and then the Korean War—old schools, old hospitals, old houses, blighted city areas, rural slums, limited water supply, air pollution. Each year increases the backlog. Estimates put our needs for public services of all kinds at a figure as high as nine billion dollars. Possibly it is more.

Finally, we are faced with the aggressive pressure of Russia. The largest single load our economy bears is the defense budget. Nor is the Soviet challenge only military. Their program of trade and aid to underdeveloped areas will increase as Soviet growth (and, let us hope, disarmament) releases more resources for their campaign to win the uncommitted and strategic areas. Our basic research, too, must be accelerated, if we are not to see Russian military teams winking at us from every planet.

Russian advances in production and increased economic assistance are bound to increase the attraction of the Communist system in the decisive underdeveloped areas. And this may do something else: having assumed our superiority for so long, for the Russians to overtake us in the economic sphere will be a greater shock to the American people than Sputnik and Lunik, and leave us confused, uncertain, and even more vulnerable to half-truths and false prophets—just when what we need to hear above the old cacophony of politics and business is the clear, clean, astringent note of the trumpet.

In one sense America has less difficulty in answering this challenge—which, it seems to me, requires an annual growth rate of 3 percent to 4 percent—than any other nation on earth or in history. In terms of the physical components of growth—materials, manpower, installed capacity, managerial capacity and technical skills—we have all of them in vast amounts and any we do not have we can import. We have already seen—in such crises as the Korean War—that production can be greatly expanded in our economy, once we decide to do it. The task of achieving a smaller but steadier expansion is certainly not beyond our powers.

Perhaps the answer lies in administrative mechanics. Maybe, for instance, the task of plotting the economy's broad course needs some strengthening of the President's economic advisers or the substitution of a national economic advisory council with members drawn from the main interests in the economy. It could be so. But for my part I think the key lies buried far deeper than this; I suspect we will find it in that system of values which

I mentioned earlier, and I further suspect that it is the lack of will, not way, which is keeping us from attaining the growth we need right now.

How do you go about acquiring a new set of values? I must confess that I am not sure. But I am certain that the first step is the stripping away of outworn prejudices and misfitting notions which prevent us from seeing the need for something new. So while we are "thinking greatly," I am going to do a little hoping greatly—that in the future the attitudes of business will not be entirely determined by pre-existing prejudice and incendiary rhetoric about the American way of life, while the Soviet way of life creeps across the earth. Is it too much to ask business to help us graduate from the nineteenth century, to throw off the semantic shackles of the dear, dead past, and get into position to meet the full scale of the real and rising attack on our way of life?

In this matter of achieving economic growth, I can see at least three battered and shopworn articles of clothing which the American businessman is still insisting on wearing: his notions on inflation, on the role of government in the economy, and on the real purposes of his business.

Let us start with inflation. It is obvious that rising prices are a real danger, and policies for dealing with them successfully offer one of the greatest challenges to democratic capitalism. Unhappily, however, the exaggeration, misstatement and fallacy which have beset the discussion of this issue often make it an exercise not of reason but of ideology.

In the first place, we are *not* on the verge of a runaway inflation as the recent propaganda would have us believe. To suggest that we are, shakes people's confidence further and encourages the very inflation against which it is supposed to warn us. Although there had been little price inflation for more than a year by early 1959, government financing was acutely embarrassed and our gold was draining away.

Another common cry is that the value of the dollar has fallen by more than half in the last fifty years. Certainly it has—but over the same period the economy has grown fourfold and the vast majority of Americans have many more dollars to spend. It is growth, startling growth, that has raised our living standards to their present unequaled height. Those who fear inflation to the point of stopping growth might be able to maintain the present living standard. But they would ensure that it grew no further.

Perhaps the most encrusted fallacies cling around the idea that only government spending is inflationary. This bit of nonsense we hear repeated over and over by top officials in industry and government. "We must hold down the federal budget," they wail, "because government spending is inflationary." This theme even bids fair to replace that tired old howl of the pessimists and the "antis": "We are spending ourselves into bankruptcy!"

The fact is that in a state of accelerating demand there is no mystic difference between *public* and *private* expenditure. A government order for a tank or a private order for a tractor have an identical effect on the demand for steel, machine tools, skilled labor, and so forth. Either public or private bidding can cause an inflationary movement. The government sparked growth—and inflation—in 1950 because of the Korean War. Private industry sparked growth—and inflation—in 1955 by expanding investment. Yet the mythical distinction between public and private spending still dominates our minds.

I suppose this is just the latest blossom on the hardy old idea that all public spending is bad and all private spending good. But the crucial question in assessing both the inflationary impact of an expenditure and its "goodness" or "badness" is: "What is the money being spent on?" and not "Who is spending it?" We—and businessmen particularly—need to look at public spending objectively, judging each item by where it is going and what we are buying with it. Education, personal security, a decent urban environment, and, today, survival in a threatened world—are these not more vital than the hairdos, the cosmetics, the drinks and tranquilizers, the chromium-encrusted cars and amusements which belong to the area of private spending?

In America more is spent per head on advertising than on education. A starlet can earn in a month five years' salary of a schoolteacher. Shining new cars stand beside gutters often choked with the refuse of a careless, wasteful people. Multiply your own instances. In fact, as Professor Galbraith has reminded us, the private sector is so well stocked that we have to go to unparalleled lengths of persuasion to keep goods moving and persuade the public to develop wants they never knew they had.

It seems a little ludicrous to hand over such vital human needs as security, education and a wide range of welfare services to the public purse because they are so vital, and then proceed to starve them simply because they are public. I am not saying, of course, that all government spending is good. What I am saying is that most of it is good, and that you will not find all the extravagance on the public side by any means.

In other words, inflation is not caused simply by government spending or simply by private spending. Before the First World War, when there were no large taxes, no large government spending, no deficits, no debt, and no unions to speak of, the average increase in inflationary pressure was just over 2 percent a year. This average is

higher than in the last decade if you exclude 1950 and
1955. But then, if you exclude those years, you also get
very little growth. We have achieved fairly stable prices
recently—incidentally, simultaneous with a thirteen-bil-
lion-dollar government deficit—but at the cost of stag-
nancy. If private production falls off by over 20 percent, government obviously can spend a lot before all
the slack is taken up and pressure begins to mount again.

So the conservatives offer us sound money, but do not
add that we may have to be content with, say, a 1 percent
rate of growth. The liberals offer us a 5 percent rate of
growth, but discount the risk of a 2 percent to 3 percent
annual inflation.

As for the business community, the weight of its influence has been on the side of security and stability rather
than enterprise, opportunity and growth. It has rarely
even tried to find an answer to the stubborn problem of
how to achieve adequate growth *and* stability. So far, its
only suggestion has been slacks and recessions to "shake
out prices." But in this last recession, some prices, particularly in industries of highly organized labor and im-
perfect competition, continued to go up. Nor do slack
times do very much to make good the backlog of public
needs. Above all, by recessions we export the instability of
capitalism for all to see. Rhodesia and the Congo have had
to endure close to a 50 percent fall in copper prices; the
primary material areas have all suffered comparable and
unsettling price losses which quickly cancel out our economic aid. In short, the remedy of recurrent recession is
no remedy and brings on other maladies just as grave.

We could, I believe, restrain the pressure on prices gen-
erated by the full use of our resources if we were ready to
exercise some self-restraint on wage and price increases.
Other democratic communities have done it. In Holland
and Sweden, the trade union movement agreed on at least

two occasions to accept lower wages at a time of international pressure on the country's balance of payments. Germany's price stability during the period of rapid growth after 1948 was due in part to the restraint shown by German labor. Are voluntary wage freezes and price reductions, especially in times of high profits, beyond our economic statesmanship in the inflation struggle? And certainly long, crippling strikes in basic industries are a severe indictment when we are in competition with the most powerful and disciplined opponent in our history.

If restraint is not forthcoming from the parties involved, what then? Are we helpless—with so much at stake? If you businessmen do not come up with some better answer than recurrent recession you will grievously embarrass capitalism, and "the public" will produce a solution—acting through government. And that answer will be more government, not less.

Another ideological blinder which limits our vision and sharply reduces our ability to make sound, objective decisions is the old, familiar refrain that any government supervision spells "socialism" and the ruin of free enterprise.

Socialism is the public ownership of the means of production, and no one is proposing that. But as we use the word, it seems to be any government authority we do not like. Of course, things we like—tariffs, subsidies, mail concessions, support prices, tax write-offs, depletion allowances and government aids to particular groups—are rarely denounced as "socialism," except perhaps by the group's competitors.

A farsighted government policy, designed to strengthen our country, improve our education, rebuild our cities, extend our services and ensure a steady growth in our productive capacity, far from being the enemy of private enterprise, is the precondition of capitalism's successful

competition with communism. It is the ally of free enterprise because it creates and maintains the climate within
which individual initiative can flourish. Consciously designed to release individual enterprise and provide a well-
nourished garden within which it can flower, public
action can be private enterprise's greatest benefactor. I
will go further and say that government is the indispensable ally of individual enterprise.

Actually only once has private enterprise been in danger of extinction in America. That was in 1929 when,
without taxes, big government, big deficits, or big unions,
it all but killed itself. Its prestige was vastly increased
by the bursting growth of the Second World War. And
after the government-sparked expansion resulting from
Korea, we got not socialism but four or five of the best
years private enterprise has ever had—and even a Republican administration! Similarly, European enterprise was
rescued from the stagnation of the twenties and thirties
by a plan launched at Harvard by a great American,
George C. Marshall. As a result, socialism has receded
in Europe, and public ownership is being abandoned
even by socialists.

Intelligent government action is not, I repeat, the
enemy but the essential complement of effective private
enterprise, and it is all the more imperative when we are
confronted by the central planning of the Soviet Union.
If government's functions are growing, so are the com-
plexities of our life, the crowding up of our country, and
our involvement in the world. A Jeffersonian dream that
"the best government is the least government" belongs
to a century when America was isolated and empty.
Today it could leave us defenseless before a challenge
neither Jefferson nor any of the founding fathers could
have possibly foreseen.

In the business world, it is not the rise of big government that gives you problems you never had or never faced up to before. In reality what you face is the forces that bring big government about. This is a big world. We have big enemies. The interests in our own country—of management and labor—are big, too, and could well become "overmighty subjects" and restore the confusion and enmity of the old feudal monopolies. In all this, government big enough to meet its responsibilities is a condition of survival. We live, day in, day out, with the great challenges of the world at large and with the great perplexities at home of a vastly increasing population. We must not be afraid of and we cannot get along without government built to their scale.

I do not ask you to agree with all I have been saying. I realize that one man's cliché can be another man's conviction. And surely there will always be sharp disagreement about the relation of government and citizens, corporate or individual. But I am deeply concerned by what I interpret as a fixation in the business community, that government is a "bad thing." Like any fixation, this one is risky at any time. In this moment, it is dangerous. Look back through history and you will find that the most penetrating and subversive attacks always come up, as it were, on the blind side, in the area where rigidity and complacency and prejudice have taken the place of thought and questioning and adaptability. Under the Manchus, no Confucian gentleman would concern himself with the scientific nonsense of the alchemists. The formidable increase in Western power based on science and technology was disregarded because science was held in such low repute. Significantly, today it is precisely by the bold use of government that the Communists challenge us most gravely—spending more proportionately on arms, aid, education and research because government can so allot the nation's resources. We shall not change this challenge simply by rejecting the instruments our foes are using. Many of us dislike the thought of government as passionately and irrationally as the Confucians rejected science. Perhaps this is the very reason why we should be ready to give it a long, new look.

Finally, a word about the purposes of a business enterprise. In the past, businessmen have driven rails across a vast continent, tamed a wilderness, released a flood of goods and services by paying primary attention to their own self-interest. That personal concern, intertwined as it was with the success of the companies they set up to gratify it, did the job of the day—though not without exacting its price.

But the rule in today's world is that man's larger interest is everywhere breaking in upon his immediate short-term interest and overriding it. This applies to business, just as to the other concerns of people. This is the logic of a unifying, contracting world, where time and distance become daily shorter; and if we deplore it, we still cannot turn the tide back. Because you are now more than ever dependent on your environment, one in which "rugged individualism" is an illusion, you will increasingly have to resolve your conflicts on the basis of what is best for that environment. Or, to put it bluntly, what is best for society. Like it or not, the business of the modern corporation is society. And smaller businesses, which are less obviously concerned with the whole life of their stockholders and suppliers, workers and customers, will increasingly find that their business, too, is society.

I do not need to say here how much that society needs the talents of the businessman. He has a gift for realism. His ideas are constantly tested by action, and he never gets far away from the practical. His motive is fundamentally optimistic. He has a rare capacity to resist adversity, and to keep coming back to the job until it is somehow done. He has drive and courage, when they are aroused and the incentive is good.

It is the incentive that counts, of course. Ours is an incentive system, which is the businessman's way of saying this is a system of individual men and women who are not compelled but who choose to do what they wish to do. But there are many kinds of incentive. Your incentive, after all, is what you decide it will be. It can be profit. It can be power. It can also be the satisfaction of making a humane mark on your time, of building a better life for the people and the community around you. These are incentives, too, if you will make them so. They are also values that society desperately needs. And they are values which people in distant places, who have more to do with our destiny than we like to think, hold higher than we always have.

America, for the first time in history, has built a productive system operated for the benefit of all the people, speaking by and large, and not for the privileged few. Considering the tenacity of privilege down through the centuries, and the many areas where it still holds unequal sway, this is an achievement on the heroic scale. The builder of this new type of system was business. But business did not think it all up. The American political system gave it its sense of direction, and there were sometimes terrible strains as the two pulled against each other.

Some may say, given my peculiar background, and because of the relationship between the two systems, that what I mean is that businessmen should get into politics. This topic is, I know, a very lively one in the business community today. As a matter of fact, it could be the latest fad, succeeding "human relations" and "management development." To some extent, I *am* saying this. You bear a heavy responsibility for the Republic's well-being and democracy's survival. The immediate means by which this is achieved—the arena of decision making —is government, and the machinery of choosing the government is politics. The health of both is the first business of every businessman, like every other citizen. But by "getting into politics" I am not recommending that you participate in order to push some particular economic viewpoint or the special interests of your company or industry. What we need, and better have a good deal more of, quickly, is concern for the *national* interest, and not the selfish interest of business, labor, farmers or any single economic, racial or religious group.

But what *is* the national interest? All of us, of course, have a slightly different view on that question, as we see readily when the issues of the day are fought out. The difficulty with the business community is that its concept of the public interest is so often limited to individual companies or at most to business as a whole. Consequently, the intellectuals and the politicians, not the businessmen, have taken the lead in shaping national thinking on public affairs. You have, in a sense, abandoned the field. Instead of putting the labor of thought into the job of articulating your views on the shape of American society, your time is spent with your lawyers and your lobbyists and your public relations officers on how to argue "your side" of the case. And you complained because "someone else" was creating a bad public image of American business.

So I am saying "participate in politics," but I am saying, even more, "beware of your heavy responsibility in our system, think through your real objectives, and evolve a vision of the America you would like to see that must take account of considerations above and beyond the success of any business."

Twenty-eight years ago, Alfred North Whitehead stood

before an audience here at the Harvard Business School and talked of the role of what he called the business mind. "Mankind is now in one of its rare moods of shifting its outlook," he said. And in this new perspective, "the motive of success is not enough. It produces a short-sighted world which destroys the sources of its own prosperity." Then he came to his point, and the point of this book. "We must not fall into the fallacy," he said, "of thinking of the business world in abstraction from the rest of the community." And he defined the aims of business in this epic phrase: "The general greatness of the community."

That says it.

Today's Most Fateful Fact

I think Bernard Shaw once said that he never resisted temptation because he had found that the things that were bad for him did not tempt him. I wish I could say the same. But I can't. I find honorary degrees always tempting, and often bad for me: tempting because we all —even ex-politicians—hope to be mistaken for scholars, and bad because if you then make a speech the mistake is quickly exposed.

This is my predicament here today. I am honored, and you have to listen to a speech. It hardly seems fair.

I thought—as all visiting Americans do—to talk to you about Canadian-American relations which are in one of our cyclical periods of irritation. But I have changed my mind because, like most family relationships, ours are so intimate and so involved that analysis is difficult. Not long ago I found Canadian confirmation for this in some words of the editor of the Victoria *Times:*

McGill University conferred the degree of Doctor of Letters, *honoris causa,* on Governor Stevenson at the graduation exercises on May 29, 1959. After the ceremony he delivered this speech to the commencement audience on the campus at Montreal.

"All the current wrangles of the border—trade, investment, seaway tolls, Columbia River electric power, farm surpluses, and the rest—represent for us Canadians only one thing, precious beyond economic calculation. So far we have been unable to articulate that thing clearly.

"We know what it means just the same. The whole problem of the border today—as always since the American Revolution—is that our neighbors *don't* know what it means, and won't bother to find out."

I think Mr. Hutchinson is right. We Americans mostly *don't* know and we ought to find out about our closest friend and neighbor and biggest customer. But I wonder if Canadians know as much about the United States as they should, too? Perhaps we ought to appoint a joint commission of international psychoanalysts to help us. And if they started to work today, I would like to make two or three suggestions for better understanding of the United States in Canada.

In the first place, it seems to me that Canadians, like other friends abroad, sometimes speak as if they thought the United States should always act promptly and decisively to satisfy their needs and complaints, regardless of the needs and wishes of American voters. They don't expect their own governments to behave the same way, and are fully aware that domestic political pressures limit the actions of their governments. For our government to behave as they suggest, it would have to be, in effect, a dictatorship, unresponsive to the opinion and desires of its own voters and able therefore to take prompt, decisive action abroad. But would Canada prefer that kind of a neighbor rather than the present one with all of its faults and weaknesses?

Another point I would ask our friends, and especially our neighbors, to remember is that the American system

of government was designed primarily for the efficient
compromise of conflicts between the states and the various sectional interests—economic, racial, religious, etc.
At that time an effective scheme for composing internal
differences was not only sensible but essential to the unification and survival of the sprawling infant country. The
system was not designed for rapid, decisive action in the
realm of foreign affairs. In those days we had few foreign
affairs and wanted less. But now our internal differences
are perhaps less urgent, while our external problems have
become infinitely complex and acute.

Our system may be obsolete, but, as Canadians will
understand, any social-political system, especially in a
democracy, is subject to a constant time lag. It can adjust
to new circumstances and demands only gradually and
painfully. Yet in the United States we have made many
adjustments in the past twenty-five years—some very far-
reaching—and I think it could be argued at least that no
other nation has shown greater flexibility and capacity for
growth.

It remains true, however, that we are not adjusting as
rapidly as we should, and *must,* in this period of bewildering and fast change in the world, and to match the swift-
ness, certainty and secrecy of the dictatorships. But is it
unreasonable of us Americans to expect, on this score,
some of the patience and understanding which you Canadians expect of us?

I would like to suggest, too, that sometimes our friends
ask too much of us. Some Canadians, for instance, sound
as if they would like us to solve their surplus wheat problem for them when we can't solve our own. The fact is
that even if our political system were not hobbled by
built-in structural and historical defects we could hardly
meet the political and economic demands upon us from
all sides, no matter how much we want to be helpful. We

are neither that wise nor that rich. We cannot supply, for instance, the massive capital investment which has been so essential to Canada's growth and is now needed so badly by all the underdeveloped countries.

And that brings me to what I really wanted to talk about: the things we will have to do together, the things that unite us, and the great unfinished business of this generation of Canadians and Americans who share the values of Western society, of which McGill University is one of the greatest repositories.

In free nations, where no strict ideology is imposed from above, there are recurrent times of ferment and questioning. These are always times of turmoil and confusion. Old ideas are discarded, new directions sought, and sometimes in the midst of it all, it is not altogether easy to perceive the main areas of decision and the proper scope of the debate.

Little more than a century ago, such a phase of questioning and revaluation was in full swing in Britain. The first onrush of the industrial revolution had changed the face of the land. It was a world of inhuman working hours, of child labor, of poverty herded into vast insanitary cities. And all this coexisted with great wealth and comfort for a few. "Two nations," wrote the wise Disraeli, of "privilege and the people," of "wealth and poverty," live side by side. Charles Dickens gave these "two nations" life and breath in his imperishable novels. Reformers—Lord Shaftesbury, the Christian Socialists, the free churches, the dogged forerunners of the labor movement —fought the widespread idea that no reform or intervention was possible since *laissez faire* had been preordained by an all-seeing Providence. And—ominously—Engels fed the evils of infant industrialism into the incendiary imagination of Karl Marx. Some decades afterwards a similar ferment was at work in America, sparking the re-

forming energies of William Jennings Bryan, Theodore
Roosevelt, Woodrow Wilson and many other leaders of
our post-Civil War period.

What the reformers finally did was to create the conviction that no decent society could tolerate so wide a
gulf between the "two nations." In a hundred different
methods of analysis and reform, they sought to establish
reasonable methods of dealing with the vast problems—
and opportunities—unleashed by industrialism and by
the wealth it created but did not equitably distribute
among the creators.

I believe a comparable period of questioning and concern has opened in the West in the last decade. We face
the end of the period of unquestioned Western suprem-
acy. We face the rising claims of the vast majority of mankind. Some of the results of modernization have spread
now to the whole human race, and once again the consequence of industrialism, undirected by broader aims of
public policy, has been to recreate Disraeli's "two nations" in the world at large. One, a small minority of
comparative wealth and privilege, lives in the main
around the North Atlantic. Here in fortunate North
America its per capita annual income is from $600 to
$2,000. But the per capita income for two-thirds of hu-
manity is not more than $100. In India, the greatest
single democratic community in the world, the average is
not much above $60 a head.

Here, then, repeated on a world scale in mid-20th century, are the riches and poverty side by side of mid-19th
century England. And we would need the pen of a Dickens to paint the contrast between the comfortable dwell-
ings of a thousand Western cities and the hovels of the
miserable millions I have seen from Hong Kong to Jo-
hannesburg.

In my judgment this disparity of living standards is the

most important and fateful fact in the world today. And the worst of it is that instead of getting better it is getting worse. The rich are getting richer and the poor poorer as their population grows faster than production. The precondition of any effective world policies in the West is an imaginative understanding of the implications of this race between resources and population; of this growing gap between a small wealthy white Western minority who have modernized and the vast majority of mankind who have not.

Once again I believe our situation resembles the 19th century. Then our forebears discovered that charity by individuals was not a complete answer. Government action, financed by the community as a whole, was necessary to make the basic improvements in health, housing and education without which the poorer members of society would lack the strength to raise themselves. A wider sharing in the wealth created by private industry—through better wages and working conditions—had a large part to play also.

Many anxious debates on the practicability of ever helping anyone to help himself accompanied the working out of these principles. Yet the outcome of the debate was the decision to achieve "the general welfare." And from it has arisen a society which, no doubt, has its flaws and blemishes but which in scope, opportunity—and, let us add, consuming power—has no equal in human history.

This outcome should encourage us now that we are involved in a new and much more complex version of the old debate. We must see that the problem of wealth and poverty in the world at large cannot be solved by handouts from individual states. Charity, with all its uncertainty and intermittence, is not the issue. Our task, as the wealthy members of world society, is to link our resources to a systematic, long-term program of education and basic development which will give the world's masses the opportunity to help themselves and bring them into effective social and economic partnership with the more developed communities. And nothing, I think, would be more appropriate than that the beneficiaries of the Marshall Plan of ten years ago should now join with America and Canada in a comparable effort for the less developed areas.

In this process I believe the basic test must be need and ability to absorb capital usefully, just as need, not virtue, has been the test inside Western society. India, for example, is close to the economic "take off" point of self-sustaining investment. It is well provided with trained administrative and technical staff and has in addition an expanding, enterprising, private sector. All this gives the hope that a really imaginative effort in India would be successful.

I would like to add that the problem is not one of government policy alone. Now—as in the 19th century debate—private enterprise has a pivotal part to play. It is concerned, rightly concerned, for the security of its investments and its returns in underdeveloped areas. It seeks reasonable guarantees, but I would like to see those guarantees worked out so that, in return for security, private firms working abroad give assurances of worker training, promotion to managerial responsibility, local directorships and the building up of a solid body of local investors and savers. All American companies may not have been as alert as they might be to these pre-conditions of responsible operation abroad. But attitudes are changing like the times and they are the chief means by which private industry can do more than simply contribute to economic development.

So, our new and common task is to assist in the search for internal stability, economic growth, and external security—without interventions which outrage national feelings and lead to a greater vulnerability to Communist agitation. It is a task of immense delicacy and immense urgency and on it turns, I believe, the future of the un-committed world. We will have to think of it with the same, or a greater, sense of urgency that we think of our military defenses.

The passing of the old colonial age has been so sudden and the emergence of the new post-colonial phase so fraught with new risks and dilemmas that it is not sur-prising to find the Western powers uncertain and fum-bling in this first decade of the new era. The changes in thought and habit which it demands on both sides of the Atlantic are vast. In the normal rhythms of history they would have demanded scores of years, even centuries, to emerge. Now they must be learned overnight. Small won-der, then, that we blunder and hesitate.

In the United States we shall have to recover from the illusion of effortless security and wealth which a fortunate 19th century, shielded by British power, has taught us to regard virtually as a natural right. We have to learn that there is no safety now in isolation, no safety in drift or self-deception, that no single "solution" or formula or declaration will rid us of the need of having a foreign policy at all.

All of us are involved. All the nations enlisted in the cause of freedom must, I fear, face years of joint responsi-bility, of working patiently with each other in pursuit of joint solutions, not despairing at early setbacks, not re-joicing too soon, but recognizing that world order is not made in a day or sustained with half thoughts and half measures.

Canada is uniquely endowed to set the issues in their right perspective—both on the side of the donors and of the recipients of assistance. I think it essential that our efforts should be international and multi-national. Few nations are better placed to set that ideal consistently before us. Canada has its part in every international grouping of consequence. Its role in the United Nations has been outstanding. It is a respected member of the Colombo Plan group, an elder daughter of the Commonwealth. Its links with the United States are—in spite of or perhaps because of recurrent conflicts of interest—the model of neighborliness. And its two cultures—English and French—give it special links with the European community. The channels of communication open to Canada thus branch out in every direction and the influence it has exercised through all of them has, I believe, been outstandingly generous and constructive.

All this makes me hope that, in the debate ahead, Canada will not be slow to use its influence, particularly in Washington and London where its voice is so eagerly attended to, to remind the statesmen of other wealthy and fortunate countries that good fortune is a responsibility, not a right or privilege.

But, equally, Canada has a vital word to say to the underdeveloped nations. For Canada still has vast untapped resources and needs outside capital to advance. It can underline to others the fact that capital assistance from abroad, public or private, does not destroy independence or lessen dignity or weaken in any way a nation's essential right to be itself and to speak its mind.

Equally, its membership in a commonwealth of nations drawn from every creed and color has not lessened its effectiveness. On the contrary, this association gives it contacts, understanding and sympathies not open to nations who have thrown off or never known the Commonwealth's friendly association between equal powers.

I trust, therefore, that Canada will make its contribution to the world's great debate tirelessly and generously;

that the vision it has shown in so many of its post-war policies will continue to give light to all of us as we grapple with the hazards and the opportunities that lie ahead for the whole family of man.

And now, before I bid you goodbye, let me add a word to the graduating classes who are about to leave this place.

I think you are fortunate to live in this stirring time of revolution.

I know you are fortunate to have lived in this famous community of scholars.

Here at McGill your education has begun. But it has not finished—and when you leave I hope you will remember why you came, and the insights that were opened for you here in this treasury of the Western culture.

And I hope that you will take away with you:

A remorseless respect for free inquiry;

Contempt for tyranny over the mind or person of man; and

Reverence for things you cannot see.

Improving Education—A Free People's Responsibility

I was flattered by your invitation to make the keynote speech at this convention—in part because I thought I was through with keynotes and conventions. But for me who knows so little about education to talk to you who know so much makes me very uneasy. And at the moment I feel as unsupported and insecure as Hillaire Belloc's water beetle:

> Who travelled on the water's face
> With ease, celerity and grace;
> But if he stopped to try and think
> Of how he did it, he would sink!

You have asked me to speak to the subject of "Improving Education—A Free People's Responsibility." Certainly the improvement is imperative, and certainly it is the responsibility of all of us; because all of us, in one way or another, are teachers and teach ourselves and others. Parents are teachers. Churchmen are teachers. Editors

Address to National School Boards Association, San Francisco, California, January 26, 1959.

are teachers. Friends are teachers. Even politicians should be teachers.

But our chief concern today is with the part of teaching that goes on in the public schools where the shape of the future is cast.

The basis for those schools was laid down in a former era when our national air was charged with promise. America was to be a new Eden. And the individual American was to be a new Adam—granted a second chance to raise a new breed of men who would liberate and purify mankind. Here there would be built a society unlike any the world had known. It would stand for the natural equality of all men, the inalienable dignity of every soul, the sacredness of conscience, the worth of labor, and the obligation of those who govern to manage for the common good the offices entrusted to their care.

This being the heroic hope, the plainest citizen was not long in seeing how and why its realization depended on public education. Let me read from "A Plea for Public Education," drawn up in 1830 by the Philadelphia Working Men's Committee:

"The original element of despotism is a monopoly of talent, which consigns the multitude to comparative ignorance and secures the balance of knowledge on the side of the rich and the rulers. If then the healthy existence of a free government be . . . rooted in the will of the American people, it follows as a necessary consequence, of a government based upon that will, that this monopoly should be broken up and that the means of equal knowledge (the only security for equal liberty) should be rendered, by legal provision, the common property of all classes."

When plain workingmen could think in these terms, when they demanded a wedding between liberty and learning, freedom and enlightenment, fate itself was bound to be kind to such vision. And so it was. It gave the American an open continent whose rich natural resources held out the promise of material bounties to come. It gave him two oceans as a shield behind which he could experiment, free from outside intrusion. It augmented the ranks of the original settlers with waves of vigorous immigrants who made their difficulties the source of their ideals, and who thought of success as but a down payment on tasks yet to be performed.

The performance of the early American often fell short of the idealized vision he had of himself and his mission. But on balance, America's solid achievements in cultivating the moral and material environment of the New World, captured the imagination of humanity everywhere. Wherever men felt the stirring of a will to remake themselves, it was to America that they looked for a guiding light.

But if this was true in the past, it is only a qualified truth today. In our national conscience, we have, I think, an even keener sense about social injustice than was the case with our forebears. Yet the ironic fact is, that we no longer hold a world-wide monopoly over the meaning of human progress and the way to attain it. Our Communist adversaries challenge our claim everywhere. At every point of human endeavor they exhibit the same restless drive we associate with the generations of earlier Americans who sacrificed the comforts of the present, that they or their children might reap larger benefits later on.

The Russians have a saying that "with good schools and hard work we will earn our place on the earth—and on the moon, too!" The zeal of the Russians for education, and their progress in converting an illiterate, backward, agrarian society into a literate, advanced, industrial state in little more than a generation, has been a spectacular achievement. It has not gone unnoticed anywhere in the world, and is profoundly attractive to the poor, less developed nations where illiteracy is still a curse.

Yet the Russians are dissatisfied with their system of education. Just as we are waking up and examining theirs, they are re-examining theirs and making basic changes. Already competitive beyond anything we know, they are making it more so. They told me that too many of those with university educations are unwilling to work with their hands, and think manual labor beneath them. So instead of ten years of pre-college education, the rulers in the Kremlin are changing it to eight, followed by two years of work in farm or factory. During the two work years, those who are "patient and industrious" and demonstrate a "thirst for learning" will be allowed to go to school part time. If they persevere at both work and studies, they can qualify for higher education after the two-year work interval.

There is one exception to this new system: those who apply themselves during the first eight years and show exceptional ability in music, the arts and mathematics, will not be required to put in two years on a farm or in a plant. But for all the others, advanced education will have to be earned on the job. And the effect will be to reduce and upgrade those who go on to higher education.

What the Russians propose to prevent is what we all know so well—that around 30 percent of our students have no purpose in higher education and only take up time of the teachers and hold back the more gifted.

It is well to remember that in Russia there is no problem of motivation. Heretofore education has been the only road to material success and distinction in Soviet society—a society that puts the members of the Academy of Sciences, the professors, artists and intellectuals at the very top of the economic and social structure, both in pay and public respect. But we in our fortunate country have many roads to success. And that very fact has doubtless diminished the value that we place on education, and often encouraged the average student to "get by" rather than to excel.

Is this attitude then more a product of our culture and our varied economic opportunities than of some defect in our educational system? And if so, what can the school boards and you educators do to create a better public understanding of the importance of education, irrespective of material rewards?

Dr. Robert Hutchins, who has never been accused of flabby complacence about our education, said something last week that is worth repeating:

"History will have trouble with American education in the twentieth century. It will see a people who say they are dedicated to education and unwilling to pay for it. It will see an educational system that delivers less education per dollar than almost any other, saying that all it needs is more money. The people and the educators are united only in this: they both want education without pain, either intellectual or financial. History will find it hard to explain how a nation that *is* one, a nation in which the political subdivisions have almost no relation to social or economic life and very little to political life, can entrust its future to these subdivisions by relegating education to them. History will smile sardonically at the spectacle of this great country getting interested, slightly and temporarily, in education only because of the technical achievements of Russia, and then being able to act as a nation only by assimilating education to the Cold War and calling an education bill a defense act.

"We might as well make up our minds to it. If our hopes of democracy are to be realized, every citizen of this country is going to have to be educated to the limit of his capacity. And I don't mean trained, amused, exercised, accommodated or adjusted. I mean that his intellectual power must be developed."

And that is your responsibility—you who are members of our school boards and charged with developing the thirst for learning and excellence of our young people. I don't envy your job. I know none more difficult, more exacting, more necessary. You have both the anti-intellectualism of so many communities, the inertia of so many pupils, and the poverty of so many school districts to overcome.

I wish you well—my future, my children's and yours are at your mercy and in your hands—far more of it is in your hands than in the hands of the Army, Navy, Air Force or Foreign Service, because if *you* fail *they* can't save us.

Admittedly, American education has had serious defects. I suppose it is because we as a people have never given the education of our young a top priority in our sense of values. Nor is education at the top of the list of alternative uses to which our tax dollar can be put. In the uses to which we can put our individual time, thought and energy, the problems of education have never had priority. The reason why our scholars and educators don't enjoy the social and economic status which most countries —especially the Communist—have accorded them is that education has never commanded the status which it merits.

Why is this? Now that we have been jolted into a realization of our inadequacy, why do we find it so difficult to cope with the problem?

The political fact is that education is a national problem which, alone among our national problems, is not handled on a national basis. Such universal problems as security and defense are treated nationally. The Govern-

ment studies the needs, appropriates the money, raises
the revenue and administers the program. But the governmental function of education has been left to the lo-
cality, to the separate community, to the separate school
board.

The fear of surrendering to centralized control the
responsibility for the education of our young is, I think,
still valid. Because in a vast country like this, the further
you remove the responsibility for education from the lo-
cality, the more you endanger the interest and concern
and the sense of responsibility of the individual citizens
in the community. And what we desperately need is more,
not less individual concern for education. Indeed I think
this need transcends classrooms, teachers and all other
school needs.

So our schools are a great national problem incapable
of a national solution. And the deficiencies of our schools
are nothing new. As Governor of Illinois, I was struggling
with them ten years before Sputnik—that brazen angel
which at last disturbed our slothful slumber.

You know better than I what the urgent needs are and
what all the critics of the American schools—the Educational Policies Commission, the White House Conference, the Rockefeller Report, and all the other reports—
say we must have for survival. I don't want to talk about
the need for more classrooms, for more counseling and
guidance, for better opportunities for the exceptional
student, and for better instruction in mathematics,
sciences and languages. I know, too, that an improvement
in the working conditions of teachers, in their compensation, in their social status, is demanded in every report
and every speech on education.

And I know, too, that to bring about these improvements there must be a substantial breakthrough in educational financing. I have talked about it during every

Congressional election in recent years—and even more emphatically during some recent Presidential campaigns!

It is often said that we are now offering much more schooling of a more expensive sort to very many more pupils than was the case fifty years ago. Yet the truth is that, compared to all other public expenditures, the ratio of what we are spending on education is not more but very much less than was the case fifty years ago. And the further truth is, that unless we start at once to divert more of our resources to education, even our physical plant will collapse once it is hit by the present explosion in our population.

The best estimates put the bill for elementary- and secondary-school education at around twelve billion dollars. In ten years it will have to be raised to around twenty-two billion dollars. Today, the bill for higher education comes to around three billion dollars. In ten years it will have increased to around nine billion dollars—for a total rise of from fifteen billion dollars annually to thirty-one billion dollars annually. With the best will in the world, state and local governments cannot do the educational job unaided.

But it was not of these familiar themes that I wanted to speak here today. Moreover, I understand that tomorrow you are going to hear Dr. Conant's report on his exhaustive investigation of our high schools and their needs. There are, however, some other aspects of education in America which deserve, I think, more attention than they get.

One is teacher training. I will not go so far as to say "that every advance in education is made over the dead bodies of ten thousand professors." But it seems to me that we should acknowledge the unhappy fact that our schools of education and teachers' colleges in the main live in isolation from the sources of intellectual ferment in the great universities. Chancellor Kimpton of the University of Chicago has reported that these schools of education over the years have developed their courses not in psychology, but in educational psychology, not in physics, but in how to teach physics, not in history, but in the techniques of teaching history. And all this, reinforced by state licensing laws, has made the student the ultimate casualty.

In short, there has been too much emphasis on how to teach a child, rather than what to teach him. Courses in education—especially at the primary level where techniques such as how to read and write must be taught—are certainly valuable. But the emphasis must be restored to teaching teachers the solid content of history, science, English, etc., instead of the techniques of teaching.

I was interested to find this same concern in the Soviet Union, where there is widespread feeling that the pedagogical institutes were overdoing the study of methods at the expense of subject matter. But a university graduate, even one who has had no courses in education, is qualified to teach. He may then compensate for this lack by attending one of the one hundred inservice teacher training institutes. Here teachers, during free hours in the day or evening, can attend classes in their own fields or get help about specific problems. These schools are, of course, free and attendance voluntary.

Personally, I doubt if we ever again have enough teachers, let alone enough good ones. We will have to have more recourse to the new techniques of teaching by film and television. Happily, the American teacher, no longer dependent on the printed page, can now draw from a vast library of remarkable educational films to open the doors of a child's mind. At last we are learning —and so are the Russians—about the enormous potential in this teaching resource. The easiest, cheapest, best method of presenting more subjects—and sometimes the only method—is films.

Every change in education is a change in the habits of teachers. Nobody of my generation ever taught with a film or was ever taught by one. And I suspect all teachers have some vague fear of technological unemployment. The facts are, of course, that these new techniques could be used in every course in the United States without throwing a single teacher out of work. The educational demands of the present time cannot possibly be met without resorting to technology as we have in every other field when manpower was short.

I wonder if the introduction of the book seemed to the teachers of those days to threaten them with technological unemployment. Actually, the book, by helping to make possible the rapid spread of education, greatly increased the demand for teachers. The book also did what the film or TV can do: it made it possible for the teacher to increase the value of his own contribution by making it unnecessary for him to do himself what the book could do for him. If the history teacher today had to recite the contents of the textbooks, he would never get around to making his own specific, personal contribution.

But I have saved for the last what is to me the most important problem of education. Some call it "excellence" —how to make our young people want to excel in their studies; some talk about "motivation"—how to make education desirable; others complain that our education is "too soft," that it fails to challenge the talents of students.

But are they not all expressions of the same thing— the attitude of the parents and the community? Don't we always have to look to the adult community for our ideals and values? Isn't our education, like our politics, just a reflection of *us*—of the prevailing attitudes and ideals of the adult community? Won't our politics pump up a cross section of the community? Won't our schools mirror the respect for academic excellence, and the intellectual motivation of parents and community? Doesn't the curriculum, hard or soft, reflect the demands of the school board, and doesn't the school board reflect the demands of the parents, and are not the parents a cross section of the community? Isn't it the community that decides whether the school bond issue passes and the board has the money it needs? And, let's face it, don't those among us who emphasize cost too often prevail over those who emphasize value?

I read that students and their families are reluctant to borrow for education. They will buy TVs, autos, washing machines, even travel, on time and credit, but not education for their children. Is it less necessary?

And isn't Dr. Hutchins right when he says that what we too often seem to want is "education without pain, either intellectually or financially?"

A member of the Chicago Board of Education recently said to me: "A school system reflects with almost terrifying accuracy the concerns of the community it serves. If parents are interested, if children are brought up with books, the whole system shows it. Principals and teachers, of course, can make an enormous difference, but by and large the community's attitude is the controlling factor."

It has been said that "a study of the education of a people can be a clue to what a given culture considers important." The overemphasis in our schools and colleges on athletics and athletic ability at the expense of intellectual attainment wouldn't last a day without public approval—probably more accurately public demand.

And when I complain about the status of teachers in this country—that here in the healthiest, strongest, richest democracy the world has ever seen, the teacher, the intellectual, the scholar, by and large, have less prestige, status and compensation than in the Communist countries—couldn't I say the same thing about many school boards? We insist on managing our education locally; yet how much attention does the average taxpayer give to the selection of the school board? And how much respect, honor and recognition do the members get from the community?

It seems to me that education in the importance of education is the most important job of education. And, worst of all, the spurt that Sputnik gave us appears to be dying down.

I conclude that it is we the people, we the parents, we the community, that are most to blame for the failures of our education. If in his home and his environment outside the school the child is indulged, how can the school be expected to turn out a better product? The courses that are taught will not be independent of the feelings, attitudes and demands of the surrounding community. If the community wants driver education or bachelor cooking instead of Latin and mathematics, it will get it. And if colleges give scholarships to boys with coordinated bodies rather than to those with coordinated minds, what will a student value?

I think it is time we, all of us, asked ourselves some searching questions about our values, about what kind of people we really are, about who we are, as the psychologists say. If our freedom means ease alone, if it means shirking the hard disciplines of learning, if it means evading the rigors and rewards of creative activity, if it means more expenditure on advertising than education, if it means in the schools the steady cult of the trivial and the mediocre, if it means—worst of all—indifference or even contempt for all but athletic excellence, we may keep for a time the forms of free society, but its spirit will be dead.

There is no boredom or misery to equal the pursuit of distraction alone. We do not slip into happiness. It is strenuously sought and earned. A nation glued to the television screen is not simply at a loss before the iron pioneers of the new collective society. It isn't even having a good time. No society has ever spent as much as we do on drink and tranquilizers. Can one argue that this is evidence of universal fun?

But perhaps this misundersanding of the true nature of happiness and of the conditions of its pursuit is simply an aspect of something else—our misunderstanding of the real nature of freedom. I recall the words of the wise Judge Learned Hand, who warned us that freedom would not survive in our Constitution if it had already died in the hearts of the people. We shall not have a free society unless we have free men.

I doubt if any society in history has faced so great a moral challenge as ours, or needed more desperately to draw on the deepest sources of courage and responsibility. Ours is the first human community in which resources are so abundant that almost no policies lie beyond our capacities for purely physical reasons. What we decide to do, we can do. The inhibitions of poverty, lack of resources, lack of power—do not hold us back. We can accomplish what we aim at. Thus, perhaps for the first time in the world, choice, not means, ends, not instruments, are decisives.

I hope we choose to upgrade education, and quickly. For as Alfred North Whitehead said forty-three years ago: "In the conditions of modern life, the rule is absolute— the race which does not value trained intelligence is doomed. Not all your heroism, not all your social charm, not all your wit, not all your victories on land or at sea, can move back the finger of fate. Today we maintain ourselves. Tomorrow science will have moved forward yet one more step, and there will be no appeal from the judgment which will then be pronounced on the uneducated."

The City—A Cause for Statesmanship

You have assigned me an impressive title—"The American City—A Cause for Statesmanship." I despair, frankly, that any words of mine can satisfy the promise of this title, or that my grasp can equal its reach.

As for The American City: I am not expert in its problems. I confess to not even living in it, but rather as far from it as the logistics of commuting permit. I know this makes me, in the literature of the subject, a "fugitive from civic responsibility," a form of parasitical growth taking income and culture from the city, and in return only adding to the morning and evening traffic jams.

As for Statesmanship: again I pretend no expertise. If certain political adventures of mine—in my youth—may have seemed to involve pretenses of statesmanship, I recognize that issue as having been publicly settled—not once, but twice.

Yet surely the first charge upon statesmanship as it applies today to the American city is clear enough. It is the charge upon statesmen responsible for all of the cities

Address given at convention of American Council To Improve Our Neighborhoods, Newark, New Jersey, May 5, 1959.

of the world. It is that these cities be permitted to survive
—that they not become, in a chain of blinding flashes,
only smoking, gaping holes in the ground. The point does
not bear laboring. But neither may it be forgotten—lest
it become the ultimate irony that man's foregathering in
the city was to simplify his self-destruction.

But survival isn't the only problem we have in common
with the rest of the world. Urban renewal and a shortage
of housing are universal problems. I was told everywhere
from Central Asia to Leningrad that housing is the num-
ber-one problem of the Soviet Union. And I have seen the
great boom towns in the exploding population areas from
Damascus to Manila, and the new central cities that have
arisen from the ashes of London, Warsaw, Berlin. Everywhere on earth the city planners and officials are struggling with the same problems of the decay and death of
old centers and the birth and growth of new ones.

In distant places, I have, like you, often thought about
our fantastic standard of living, and that in spite of bless-
ings that exceed the grasp, even the imagination, of most
of the world's people, we in America have still fallen far
short of even arresting the spread of blight and decay in
our cities. Like you, I have often wondered how we can
hope to solve the problems of maintaining our alliances,
of meeting the Communist economic and scientific offensive, of extending a helping hand to the peoples now
searching for national identity and independence, of
standing firm against aggression anywhere, if we can't
mobilize our domestic resources to meet the needs of
day-to-day work and living.

We are not concerned just with the new low-income
and minority ghettos in some cities, nor just with real-
estate values in the downtown central business districts,
nor the bedeviled commuter, nor the costly, growing traffic
congestion, nor the general offensiveness of the urban

sprawl. The deficiencies in our schools and communal services, like parks, playgrounds, hospitals, and the ugly outcroppings of juvenile violence, are all pleading for attention and are all part of the broader task of revitalization and reinvigoration of the city as a way of life.

It is not even a renaissance we seek; rather it is the construction of an entirely new mode of living—poles apart from the Victorian city of old. What we are concerned with is the exciting, exhilarating adventure of constructing economic, financial, social and political tools to build —not a city—but a metropolis.

But to return to "statesmanship" in this context—I would define it simply as the marking and the doing of the central thing that needs to be done—finding the right key—and turning it.

If there is a key to the answers to the problems which today beset our cities, I am sure I haven't got it. I don't think there is one key. But I think of Pope's line about a key to a drawer wherein lie other keys.

Because, I suppose, many of the best years of my life have been devoted to the problems of government, the drawer I look to is the one marked "government"—government with a small g (which suddenly reminds me of Oscar Wilde's remark that nothing produces such pleasing effects as a good platitude).

Government with a small g does not mean, for me, the agencies of public government as distinguished from those of what we call business or private enterprise. I wish everyone could realize, as you do, how closely the functions of a corporation are related to "governmental" functions when—for example—a great insurance company takes over the clearing of a slum and its replacement with the facilities for decent, twentieth-century living.

The problems of the American city will be met when, and not until, we recognize that they are already and inexorably committed to the *joint* trusteeship of private enterprise and public responsibility; that they demand a shoulder-to-shoulder, two-fisted attack; that their solution depends entirely upon an alliance of private and public agencies—with each respecting its own limitations and the capacities of the other, and with each acting in support of the other.

It is equally essential to recognize that the public agencies involved operate at three levels—federal, state and local—and that there is a similar problem of distributing responsibilities among these three, with each being equipped to do its appointed part.

America has the resources, the wealth, the raw materials, the intelligence, the technical know-how, the pressing need and the driving desire to solve all the problems which have so far prevented the remaking of the cities. Statesmanship's question here is not *what* to do but *who* is to do it—and how to make an alliance among the agencies involved, as you have evidently done with such spectacular success here in Newark.

There is no point in emphasizing at an ACTION conference the stake private enterprise—including every businessman in every city in America—has in the preservation and the strengthening of the urban structure. You, more than any other group, have pointed out that what is good for the American city is good for every businessman who operates there.

Part of these returns are direct—in profit on the building projects themselves. But more and more the business community is coming to realize that urban renewal also means more customers coming in the doors, that an equity investment in a slum clearance development project represents philanthropy—at a profit. We are beginning to recognize that not only charity, but investment as well, can best begin at home, *in* homes.

I suspect that in the long run the clearing of slums will come less as the result of public concern about the people there being poor people than as a product of the business community's concern about their being poor customers. This isn't cynical. It simply recognizes the fact that it is hard to sustain public concern—except when a school burns down or a rat bites a child—in a problem which neighbors can solve by moving away from it. But businesses can't easily do that.

So business, especially big business, has a great opportunity here to make a contribution—and to make a profit.

But there are some parts of this job that just cannot be done at a profit, and therefore will not be done privately. The necessary distribution of responsibilities for city saving will not come about as long as influential groups insist that any governmental financial aid, except to guarantee mortgages, is socialist sin—which you are either against in all of its manifestations or for, all the way. For that matter we will never get our sights straight as long as influential people persist in the myth that all public spending is bad, all private spending good. I believe it was Justice Holmes who said: "I buy civilization with my taxes."

I came across, the other day, a speech I made at a Housing Day Conference in Chicago ten years ago. This line jumped out at me: "The public housing debate is over." That was shortly after, of course, the enactment under the sponsorship of Senators Taft, Wagner and Ellender, of the Housing Act of 1949—providing for the building of 135,000 public housing units a year for six years, or 810,000 in all.

But now, ten years later, only half of those 810,000 units have been built, and some of those who denounced Senator Taft as an "old Republican" have brought in a housing bill providing for no public housing at all.

Nobody "likes" public housing. It is a mark of failure, and the nation will welcome and accept the views of those critics of public housing who will develop alternatives which are constructive and realistic. But mere insistence that private enterprise can do the job without public housing is no answer—unless this insistence is backed up with action. We are entitled to say here, with a new meaning, "either put up—or shut up."

There is reason for larger satisfaction about the increasing supply of middle-income housing. I saw a few days ago in New Haven the heartening spectacle of a beautiful new city rising from the ashes of ugliness and neglect. We have in Chicago now, as you have in a number of your cities, substantial developments which confirm the willingness and ability of private capital and enterprise to carry the job of reconstruction forward if public funds are available for the preliminary clearing of the old slum areas.

I am most encouraged, incidentally, by the reports of success in leasing these new accommodations on "open-occupancy" basis, for any realistic appraisal of the housing problem must take account of the serious danger that subsidized housing will become racially segregated housing and will thereby aggravate a problem as serious as the housing problem itself.

Last week a friend of mine who has done a great deal to rebuild Chicago showed me how the private equity investment of $4,725,000 per year for ten years will produce the capital required to completely rebuild an entire square mile of slums with fine, modern living accommodations which can be rented to low-middle-income families at a fair profit. I was sobered when he added that this proposition assumes a public subsidy to acquire this land and to write it down to use value, and that these costs will run to $8,000,000 per year. Yet this is the kind of cooperative venture, the kind of public-private alliance, which alone can do this job. It appeared, for a while, that there was solid recognition of the degree of aid that would have to come from federal sources to support local urban renewal, in both its private and its public aspects. Of late, there has been considerable doubt cast on both the extent of such aid and its character or continuance. The plain fact is that those who oppose federal aid for urban renewal are actually against urban renewal. For they know full well that many of the possibilities of local revenue have been pre-empted by federal and state taxing bodies, that the largest urban centers are operating under archaic revenue authority with little hope of relief from state legislatures dominated by non-urban lawmakers. The vast sums urban renewal requires are just not available exclusively from private funds or from the local resources of the overwhelming majority of urban centers.

From administrative experience we have learned some lessons the hard way. It is clear now that the administrators of the federal program destroy the effectiveness of local authorities and discourage willing private investors when they keep changing the rules of the game, throwing out projects which were carefully devised to conform to the old rules but which don't meet the new ones. Too many of us here are familiar with the crippling effect in our own cities of arbitrary notices from Washington that all projects are to be scaled down by an arbitrary percentage. Too often the scaled-down project just doesn't make sense. Half a building is not better than none, and it is often the falsest economy to pick at a slum instead of rending a bulldozer all the way through it.

It is noteworthy, too, that these pending bills reflect the significance of the conservation principle that a dollar put into preventing urban decay is ten dollars saved in subsequent rebuilding.

Such legislation deserves support solely in terms of the human values that are involved. The juvenile delinquency a slum breeds infects a whole city. The tax bill for it—for police regulation, for fire protection, for relief payments—goes to every taxpayer.

You and I vote at each election with complacent confidence that democratic capitalism means security and the supplying of life's purposes. But our votes count no more than the votes from slum victims which are not based on that faith.

I reread not long ago the story of the twenty-one American soldiers who chose not to return from the Korean Communist prison camp but to stay with those who had captured their minds as well as their bodies. Fifteen of those "21 Who Stayed" came from slums—some in the cities, some in the country. I could only think of Bret Harte's poetic dictum that nobody shoulder a rifle in defense of a boarding house.

But, we are being told, we can't afford these things.

I would, if it were necessary, say to this that there are emergencies in which you call the doctor without asking the cost, and that cancer in our cities is such a case. When somebody starts talking about the evil of passing a burden of public debt on to the next generation it makes me want to ask if it is better to pass on a burden of slums, of ignorance, of national weakness—and ultimately greater debt. We have a way of saying about reforms and changes that they were "inevitable." But with urban renewal as with everything else—"the mode by which the inevitable comes to pass is effort."

But to support a program of full-scale renewal and rebuilding of the cities is not to be soft-hearted (which seems to me no sin); it is also to be hard-headed. I am not a budget buster. But I do believe in America's greatness, and that this greatness can be traced to bold leaders and bold enterprises and the basic notion that money invested properly and adequately will multiply wealth. And every dollar of public funds that goes into slum clearance and urban renewal will be returned to the public coffers in increased revenues.

In the face of these great needs which are also great opportunities, I hope we are ready to stop the demagogic political debate which assumes that government and private enterprise are inherently antagonistic. I hope we are now ready to accept, instead, the demanding necessity for a confident alliance of public and private enterprise in meeting the problems of the city.

Money is not enough. Indeed the wrong amount of money at the wrong time and in the wrong place may hinder rather than help our efforts to construct the city of the future. We Americans have a penchant for believing that sufficient inputs of energy and dollars can solve any problem. We rush in where angels fear to tread and frequently we profit, but sometimes we learn why the angels, in their greater wisdom, have not joined us and preferred to stay aloft. Urban reconstruction is a case in point.

Despite the laudable efforts we have been making to deal with various aspects of the problem in the generation since the New Deal began, does the sum of these parts add up to a meaningful whole? Instead of developing a comprehensive program, are we in danger of creating a patchwork, a conglomeration of temporary and short-sighted solutions to pieces of a problem which cannot be handled piecemeal? Even in that haven of generalities—a preamble to a federal law—we look in vain for a comprehensive statement of what we are after.

What do we want our downtown centers to become? What, in the long run, are the proper uses of the land in the "gray belt"? What kind of transportation system will best meet our needs? How do we want to use the remaining open spaces around our cities—for parks, for wild-life reservations, for industries or for the next wave of developments?

We shall have to look to groups like this for responsible, sustained help in finding the answers. But it will have to be left to the citizens of each urban community, acting through their own governments, to settle their own issues. And here we run into another familiar problem of government—the problem of too much government. At the local level the jumble of bureaus, municipalities, counties, commissions, authorities, corporations and officialdom generally has neither a sense of union nor a sense of direction. In most instances even the skeleton of a limp confederation is lacking.

At the very root of this problem is also the fact that although we have become a dominantly urban and suburban society, our political thinking and structure is still predominantly country minded. Coming from the country, I have no quarrel with rural people. But the fact is that one hundred million Americans live today in 168 metropolitan areas. This is over 60 percent of our total population. Yet in most legislatures the vote of a small town or rural citizen is worth substantially more than his city cousin's.

I know from my years as governor of a divided state how difficult this problem is. There are two sides to it. And yet there is bound to be a change. Local governments must be given the fiscal authority which the discharge of their responsibilities demands. There must be enlargement, in one way or another, of the revenue sources available to them. Gotham won't secede from

New York, nor Chicago from Illinois, but this is a serious problem and it is going to take ingenuity—and a willingness to seek out entirely new ways—to meet it.

These urban problems have today become metropolitan problems, problems that cross all lines between city and suburbs and between incorporated and unincorporated areas, problems that have no city limits.

The plain fact is that the resources on which our urban life depend—land, water and breathable air—are getting scarcer. The decisions about their use, like the decisions about transportation, are hard decisions. Any assumption that the city planners or high level commissions will devise the answers seems to me to go only halfway. For the answers, however wise, won't mean anything unless they are adopted—through the political decision-making process—by those affected by these decisions.

I know the difficulties which will be in the way of developing new machinery of decision. The sovereignties and vested interests of established local units and officialdom will be as hard to break down as they are at the national and international levels. The various suburbs which surround our major cities are already developing special ethnic and economic personalities, and this will make it harder and harder for the citizens of one area to be persuaded to submit their interests to a common vote which includes the citizens of another.

But I know, too, of the bold, effective way this problem has been met by Toronto. We are all watching eagerly the imaginative inquiry being conducted at Detroit. Other cities have taken the first essential steps toward metropolitan planning and are now looking to the possibilities of limited metropolitan government.

If building new instruments seems hopeless, then I must say that I think the other choice is to accept for our cities the fate of eternal worrying at the edges of our urban concerns, of everlasting plucking at ever broadening scabs of blight and decay; while more authority will remain at the higher state and federal levels.

A Balkanized metropolis can probably cope, in desperation, with the problems of urban survival. It can make our day-to-day difficulties tolerable. But I doubt if it can ever conceive the great plans, set the great policies, make the great decisions, which are essential if the cities are to be built and rebuilt according to the blueprints of our hopes.

I have tried to suggest that the problems of the American city demand the exercise of what is perhaps the most difficult art of democratic government: the effective mobilization of all of the forces which make up the free body politic and the free body economic—not just to make the right decisions, but also to carry them out.

There are people in the world today who say that tough public problems are best solved behind closed doors, by dictators or central committees. But in our land we dare not even reach for a goal of human improvement in disregard of human values, human judgments. The central tenet of statesmanship in a democracy is that unless the people understand it and participate in it, no long-term program can endure.

The municipality of tomorrow must be renewed in the image of people's hopes and ambitions for a better life. The values to be recreated must have a sound political and economic pedestal, but they must flow from human needs.

Thus will we build and rebuild our cities, and in so doing renew and rekindle our faith in ourselves and in the limitless creativeness of free men.

Lincoln's Faith

In the near-century since his death, Abraham Lincoln has become a symbol and much more, not only to Americans, but to all men everywhere, a symbol of many facets, many meanings.

To Americans at large he is the President who saved the Union of States from self-destruction and freed a whole race of men from human bondage. To the informed student of history, he is the foremost defender of constitutional law. At home and abroad he is proof incontrovertible of the dream that brought the first settlers to our shores and has beckoned folk from other lands ever since, the core of the American philosophy—that in a free society a man can pull himself up by his own bootstraps. Lincoln did it. And so it can be done.

But the universality of his appeal is more than that, and is found in the character of the man himself. Other statesmen have become remote in greatness—Lincoln never did. He has lived on for the people as a man—a flesh and blood and bone human being, whose greatness they can

From *The Observer*, London, February 8, 1959.

accept because they can understand his origin, his ways, his talk and his laughter.

Perhaps it is his gift for language that has kept the image clear. An avid student of Shakespeare, Byron, Burns, Lincoln spoke oftenest in parables, illustrating a point with a homely story of frontier life, or even of animals in the manner of Aesop. "God tells the truth in parables," he is quoted as saying, "they are easier for the common folk to understand and recollect." And yet his great speeches—the farewell to his townsfolk when he left Springfield, Illinois, for Washington, the Gettysburg address, the inaugurals and some of his messages to the United States Congress, soared to heights seldom approached by any other statesman in history.

However, Lincoln was more than a writer, a spokesman. What endears him in the minds of all freedom-loving people as the greatest democrat in our history—or any history—was his own faith in democracy, in the ability of the people to govern themselves. He based that faith in the Declaration of Independence, and spoke of it time and again, perhaps most succinctly on his way to Washington in February, 1861, before the New Jersey Senate. He recalled the revolutionary struggle and said:

"I am exceedingly anxious that that thing which they struggled for; that something even more than national independence; that something that held out a great promise to all people of the world for all time to come . . . shall be perpetuated in accordance with the original ideal for which that struggle was made, and I shall be most happy indeed if I shall be an humble instrument in the hands of the Almighty, and of this His almost chosen people, for perpetuating the object of that great struggle."

Lincoln regarded democracy as "the last, best hope of earth"—as that form of government which promised "that in due time the weight would be lifted from the shoulders of all men."

He saw America as the trustee for humanity, and the terrible civil war, more costly in human lives than any other war in history, as a testing of that trusteeship. The Union of States was bound together by an idea—the idea that men are fit to govern themselves—and if the Union perished, the idea would perish with it. Slavery was only a part of the issue—the excuse, but not the whole reason, for the war.

Very early in the conflict he explained his feelings to his young secretary, John Hay, saying, "For my part, I consider the central idea pervading this struggle is for the necessity that is upon us of proving that popular government is not an absurdity. We must settle this question now, whether in a free government the minority have the right to break up the government whenever they choose. If we fail it will go far to prove the incapability of the people to govern themselves."

He expressed his faith most forcibly in the ringing closing of his speech at Gettysburg: ". . . . this nation, under God, shall have a new birth of freedom—and that government of the *people,* by the *people,* for the *people,* shall not perish from the earth."

Lincoln believed firmly in social evolution, a kind of inevitability for human development, and saw the democratic form of government as the most promising environment for that evolution. "We propose to give *all* a chance," he said, "and we expect the weak to grow stronger, the ignorant to grow wiser; and all better and happier together."

Lincoln, by his own acknowledgment, derived his political beliefs mostly from Thomas Jefferson. His own contributions to democratic thought consist solely of amplifications, extensions, and masterly expressions of it. Yet it is to Lincoln rather than to Jefferson that people in general look today as democracy's foremost spokesman and exemplar. If the supreme test of a democratic leader is his democratic faith, then this judgment of the people is correct; for in this, Lincoln stands pre-eminent.

How did Lincoln arrive at this deep faith in mankind? Because he was one of them. He knew nothing of privilege; born in poverty, schooling himself, working incredibly hard for every personal advancement, he *knew* the people good and bad, ridiculous and sublime, and he believed there was more good than bad in most of them. He believed it so completely that he was willing to risk war to prove it.

And so we see ourselves in Lincoln, as he saw himself in people. That greatness in him—is there not some of it in my neighbor, myself, my son? Of course there is, we tell ourselves, for Lincoln was all of us—the spokesman for all that went before him in the building of America and everything we have fought since to preserve. And so, while statesmen come and statesmen go, Lincoln in his person and in his life work remains the greatest democrat of us all, and a continuing inspiration to all mankind.